T0150450

 REGENERATION

REGENERATION

SPIRITUAL GROWTH AND HOW IT WORKS

Emanuel Swedenborg

Introduction by Lee van Laer

SWEDENBORG FOUNDATION

West Chester, Pennsylvania

Library of Congress Cataloging-in-Publication Data
Swedenborg, Emanuel, 1688-1772.
  [Works. Selections. English. 2014]
  Regeneration : spiritual growth and how it works / Emanuel Swedenborg ;
introduction by Lee van Laer.
     pages cm
  ISBN 978-0-87785-429-6 (alk. paper)
  1. Regeneration (Theology) 2. General Church of the New Jerusalem—
Doctrines. I. Title.
  BX8729.R4S9413 2014
  234'.4—dc23
                    2014015682

"Love and the Self" was taken from Emanuel Swedenborg, *New Jerusalem,* trans. George F. Dole (West Chester, PA: Swedenborg Foundation,
forthcoming).

"Repentance" and "Reformation and Regeneration" were originally published in Emanuel Swedenborg, *True Christianity,* trans. Jonathan S. Rose,
vol. 2 (West Chester, PA: Swedenborg Foundation, 2011).

"The Role of Levels in Regeneration" was originally published in Emanuel
Swedenborg, *Divine Love and Wisdom,* trans. George F. Dole (West Chester,
PA: Swedenborg Foundation: 2003).

"Creation" was originally published in Emanuel Swedenborg, *Secrets of
Heaven,* trans. Lisa Hyatt Cooper, vol. 1 (West Chester, PA: Swedenborg
Foundation, 2008).

Edited by Morgan Beard
Design and typesetting by Karen Connor

Printed in the United States of America

Swedenborg Foundation
320 North Church Street
West Chester, PA 19380
www.swedenborg.com

CONTENTS

 INTRODUCTION

And I said to the man who stood at the gate of the year:
"Give me a light that I may tread safely into the unknown."
And he replied:
"Go out into the darkness and put your hand into the Hand of God.
That shall be to you better than light and safer than a known way."

—FROM "GOD KNOWS" BY MINNIE LOUISE HASKINS

Emanuel Swedenborg was an important influence on Western metaphysical thinking during the nineteenth and early twentieth centuries; yet, oddly enough, this influence is no longer keenly felt. That is unfortunate, because Swedenborg brought humankind some of its most extraordinary and unusual observations about the nature of its own physiology, psychology, and spirituality. Many of his ideas are timeless; they include significant insights about the human nervous system, including the nature of neurons and the functional purpose of the cerebral cortex. His doctrine of the unity of all things in a fundamental, transcendent, and infinitely creative state of divine love is echoed in the esoteric Islam of Muhyiddin Ibn 'Arabi and the contemporaneous mystical sermons of Meister Eckhart. His insistence on spirituality as a substantive material and chemical phenomenon passes through to the twentieth century, finding a comfortable home in the teachings of G. I. Gurdjieff.

Yet he did not come to his understanding through Eckhart or Ibn 'Arabi. Swedenborg proposed a detailed metaphysic based on his own unique, angelic revelations, and this was a radical departure. Eckhart, Ibn 'Arabi, and Gurdjieff *spoke* of heaven; Swedenborg reported that he had *been* there—not once or twice, but many times. His stories—repeated trips to heaven and hell, extended conversations with angels and demons, detailed information on the exact nature of the afterlife—might be construed by some as the ravings of a madman, but for the extensive evidence of his absolute and comprehensive rationality. He was a respected scientist, mining engineer, and metallurgist; he designed flying machines; and he was one of the first to propose the nebular hypothesis of planetary formation. Those who knew him reported him as a responsible, understated, and mild-mannered man; he avoided untoward displays of his clearly unusual and documented psychic abilities, and held practical, responsible positions in government offices for a major part of his life.

Many of the remarks he makes about heaven and hell are so original, and so detailed, that they compel belief. His accounts of the nature of heaven and his contention that people end up in hell only because that is where they want to be are stunning. So, too, is his pronouncement that entry to heaven is open to all, as long as their hearts are open and their intentions are good. It is fair enough to say that spiritual understanding this intelligent, liberal, compassionate, and merciful is so modern that we have not quite caught up with it in most parts of the world even today. Thus Swedenborg is a man not for his own time, or some earlier time, but for all times and for all places.

In this book, we encounter Swedenborg's understanding of spiritual transformation. This transformation is accomplished through a conscious awareness of our position and the spiritual level we are on; Swedenborg insists, like Gurdjieff, that intent is essential to humankind's inner growth and spiritual well-being, that the nature of a person's essence is paramount, and that good intentions are not enough. Like the Buddhists, he insists on a call to right action: it is not enough just to know what goodness is; one must act on it. In this way, he casts human beings in the same role that Ibn 'Arabi gives them: vicegerents of God.

A responsibility is conferred upon us; we meet this responsibility by using our understanding, or intellect, to recognize what is good and then act on it through will. Ideas such as this must be construed as common sense; as such, they easily transcend any religious context, becoming acceptable to all right-thinking human beings. One need not believe in God to believe in goodness; and one need not believe in God to do good. Even the most ardent atheists would agree that this particular baby must never be thrown out with the bathwater, lest we lose the fundamental premise of civilization and our humanity itself.

Nonetheless, this is not an atheistic book. Although Swedenborg was, at heart, a brilliant rationalist—in both scientific and religious matters—and although he imparted a detailed, intellectual structure to all of his spiritual works, they are, in the end, works of the heart. The axiom of love penetrates everything he writes; like Meister Eckhart, he sees the divine love of God at the center of the universe and at the core of everything within it. We are alive only because of love; and we can act only through love. Without this understanding, without an ever-deeper penetration of our being by divine love, even the most brilliant realization is ultimately worthless. In fact, as he points out here, genius can lead a person to hell as easily as to heaven, if no love guides it.

This collection of excerpts from Swedenborg's writings, like all of Swedenborg's books, is filled with truths imparted from a higher level. In our modern era, with a plethora of different religious and philosophical belief systems to choose from, we can think of that higher level in terms of consciousness, or as inspiration from the Muses, or as a state of being like enlightenment. Swedenborg defined his experiences in Christian terms, attributing wisdom to angelic contact and, ultimately, to God. According to Swedenborg, the angelic realms rarely communicate directly with human beings; such contact is usually forbidden, and is only undertaken in cases of necessity. The Christian Bible is, of course, filled with classic examples; but the days when angels appear in person to announce events of magnitude seem, for the most part, to be long over.

History has left us with some few recent (I use the term loosely) records of contact of that kind, notably Dante's *Divine Comedy* and Gurdjieff's *All and Everything*. And of course there is poetry; one example is the work of William Blake, who was an avid reader of Swedenborg. It is certain, however, that Swedenborg's work stands as one of the greatest records of such received wisdom. His stunning recognition of our own selfishness, with its terrifying consequences, stands forever as an essential and critical observation on the nature of human psychology, whether or not one chooses to ascribe that nature or its consequences to supernatural forces.

In short, there is so much one can be sure is right in Swedenborg's observations on spiritual transformation that one is left wondering whether he could have been wrong about anything. That question raises even deeper ones, questions that lead one to ponder one's existence and action deep into the night and early in the morning, when darkness surrounds the soul and no answers come easily.

This is a book for those hours, when we call into question everything we are and hope against hope that we will find not light, or a known path, but—instead—the Hand of God.

LEE VAN LAER
Sparkill, New York

 EDITOR'S NOTE

This volume brings together a series of writings from Emanuel Swedenborg on the process of spiritual rebirth, which he called *regeneration.*

Swedenborg published twenty-five theological volumes during his lifetime. Although his writings include much discussion of spiritual growth in the context of other topics, Swedenborg devoted chapters explicitly to regeneration in only two of his books: *New Jerusalem* (1758) and *True Christianity* (1771). Both of those works may be considered summaries of his theology, and they neatly bookend his career: *New Jerusalem* was one of the first books that Swedenborg published after completing his first and longest theological work, *Secrets of Heaven* (1749–56), while *True Christianity* was his last published book. Although *New Jerusalem* and *True Christianity* are very different in structure, in both works Swedenborg introduces the topic of regeneration by discussing a series of key concepts: will, understanding, love, faith, goodwill, freedom, and repentance. This volume begins in the same way, presenting these topics in the same order that Swedenborg used.

Swedenborg wrote in Neo-Latin—a form of Latin used in scholarly and scientific publications from the sixteenth to the twentieth centuries—and his works have been translated many times throughout the years. The excerpts here are taken from the New Century Edition of the Works of Emanuel Swedenborg, a translation series that renders his writing in modern English while preserving the clear and straightforward style of the original. However, because different translators render certain key terms in different ways, in this volume the terminology has been harmonized to help readers more easily follow Swedenborg's thought from one section to the next.

One key concept in Swedenborg's writing that is particularly difficult to translate is the Neo-Latin *charitas,* which in older translations is generally rendered as "charity." The same word, however, can also convey a sense of caring, loving kindness, or good feelings toward others; for consistency in this volume, it is translated as "goodwill." His terms *voluntas* and *intellectus,* traditionally translated "will" and "understanding," also appear that way here; however, Swedenborg's use of *voluntas* may also be translated as "volition" and *intellectus* as "intellect," "thought," or "discernment." Sometimes, too, his use of *intellectus* refers to a faculty capable of intellectual perception at a high, intuitive level.

Swedenborg frequently inserts cross-references to other sections in the same work or in his previously published works. He numbered the sections in his books to make the referenced material easier to find, and so the cross-references to his other publications refer to the section numbers—which remain uniform across almost all translations—rather than page numbers. Within this volume, Swedenborg's original cross-references have been either changed (to reflect where the text appears in this book) or deleted (if he is referring to a section that is not included here). In addition, some passages have been abridged, with the omitted material indicated by ellipses.

Readers interested in exploring Swedenborg's complete text are encouraged to consult the source material:

"Love and the Self" is from *New Jerusalem* (translated by George F. Dole, forthcoming edition), §§28–33, 54–119, and 141–47.

"Repentance" is from *True Christianity,* vol. 2 (translated by Jonathan S. Rose, 2011), §§509–66.

"Reformation and Regeneration" is also from *True Christianity,* vol. 2 (translated by Jonathan S. Rose, 2011), §§571–620.

"The Role of Levels in Regeneration" is from *Divine Love and Wisdom* (translated by George F. Dole, 2003), §§179–270.

"Creation" is from *Secrets of Heaven,* vol. 1 (translated by Lisa Hyatt Cooper, 2008), §§1–63.

REGENERATION

 # LOVE AND THE SELF

WILL AND UNDERSTANDING

We have two abilities that make up our life, one called *will* and the other *understanding*. They are distinguishable, but they are created to be one. When they are one, they are called *the mind*; so they *are* the human mind, and it is there that the entirety of our life is truly to be found.

Just as all things in the universe (those that agree with the divine design) trace their origin back to goodness and truth, so everything in us traces its origin back to our will and understanding. This is because whatever good we have depends on our will and whatever truth we have depends on our understanding. These two faculties, these twin living parts of us, receive and are acted upon by what is good and true: our will receives and is acted upon by everything that is good, and our understanding receives and is acted upon by everything that is true. Goodness and truth can be found nowhere else in us but in these faculties. Furthermore, since they are not to be found anywhere else, neither are love and faith, since love and goodness are mutually dependent, and similarly faith and truth.

Now, since everything in the universe traces its origin back to goodness and truth and everything in the church traces its origin back to the good that love does and the truth that our faith understands, and since we are human because of will and understanding, the theology [I am now presenting] deals with will and understanding as well. Otherwise we could have no clear concept of them, no solid foundation for our thinking.

Will and understanding also form the human spirit, since they are where our wisdom and intelligence are found; or, to state it in general terms, they are our life's own true dwelling.

The body, by contrast, is simply a thing that follows orders.

There is no knowledge more relevant than knowing how our will and understanding make one mind. They make one mind the way goodness and truth make a single reality. There is the same kind of marriage between will and understanding as there is between goodness and truth. That is, an instance of goodness is the actualizing of something, and truth is the manifestation of the thing that is actualized. In the same way, it is through our will that our lives are actualized, and it is through our understanding that our actualized life becomes manifest to us. This is because any instance of goodness that comes from our will takes form in our understanding and manifests itself [to our apprehension] there.

People who are focused on what is good and true have both will and understanding, while people who are focused on what is evil and false do not have will or understanding. Instead of will they have craving, and instead of understanding they have more information. Any genuine human will is receptive to goodness, and any genuine human understanding is open to truth. This means that will cannot be associated with anything that is evil and understanding cannot be associated with anything that is false—because these things are opposites, and opposites are mutually destructive. That is why anyone who is focused on something evil and therefore on what is false cannot be called rational, wise, or intelligent. Then too, the deeper levels of our minds are closed when we are evil, and those levels are where our will and understanding principally reside.

We assume that we have will and understanding even when we are evil because we say that we are willing things and understanding them, but our "willing" in that case is nothing but craving and our "understanding" is mere information. . . .

OUR RULING LOVE

Our love is our life itself. What our love is like determines how we live and therefore everything about what we are as human beings. It is, however, specifically our ruling or dominant love that makes us who we are.

That love has many loves subordinate to it, loves that derive from it. They take on various guises, but nevertheless these specific loves are inherent in the ruling love and together with it make a single domain. The ruling love is like their monarch or head. It governs them and works through them as intermediate goals, in order to focus on and strive for its own goal, the primary and ultimate of all. It does this both directly and indirectly.

Whatever belongs to our ruling love we love more than anything else.

Whatever we love more than anything else is constantly present within our thoughts and also within our intentions. It constitutes the very essence of our life. For example, if we love wealth more than anything else, whether in the form of money or in the form of possessions, we are constantly calculating how we can acquire it. We feel the deepest joy when we do acquire it and the deepest grief when we lose it—our heart is in it.

If we love ourselves more than anything else, we are mindful of ourselves at every little moment. We think about ourselves, talk about ourselves, act to benefit ourselves. In fact, our life is a life of pure self.

We have as our goal whatever we love more than anything else. We focus on it constantly in each and every thing we do. It is within our will like the hidden current of a river that draws and carries us along even when we are doing something else, because it is what animates us.

This is the ruling love that we see and examine in others, using it either to lead them or to cooperate with them.

Our quality is entirely determined by what controls our life. That is what distinguishes us from each other. That is what determines our heaven if we are good and our hell if we are evil. It is our essential will, everything we claim to be, and our nature. In fact, it is the very substance of our life. It cannot be changed after death because it is what we really are.

Everything we find pleasing, satisfying, and happy comes to us from our ruling love and answers to it. We call whatever we love pleasing because that is how it feels to us. While we can also call something pleasing that we think about but do not love, that is not a pleasure of our life.

To enjoy our love stands as what is good in our estimation, and anything we do not enjoy stands as what is bad in our estimation.

There are two loves from which arises everything that is good and true, as though from their very wellsprings, and there are two loves from which arises everything that is evil and false. The two loves that are the source of everything good and true are love for the Lord and love for our neighbor, while the two loves that are the source of everything evil and false are love for ourselves and love for this world.

These latter two loves are the exact opposites of the former two loves.

The two loves that are the source of everything good and true (which as just stated are love for the Lord and love for our neighbor) make heaven for us, so they reign in heaven as well; and since they make heaven for us they also make the church.

The two loves that are the source of everything evil and false (which as just stated are love for ourselves and love for this world) make hell for us and therefore reign in hell as well.

The two loves that are the source of everything good and true (which as just stated are heaven's loves) open and give form to our inner, spiritual self because that is where they live. However, when the two loves that are the source of everything evil and false are in control, they close and wreck our inner, spiritual self and cause us to be earthbound and sense-bound according to how much they dominate us and according to the manner in which they do it. . . .

Love for ourselves is intending benefit only to ourselves and not to others except as it is in our own interests—not to our church or country, not to any human community or fellow citizen. Love for ourselves is also being good to others only for the sake of our own reputation, advancement, or praise, so that unless we see some such reward in the good we may do for them we say at heart, "What's the use? Why should I? What's in it for me?" and forget about it. This shows that when we are caught up in love for ourselves we are not loving our church, our country, our community, our fellow citizens, or anything worthwhile—only ourselves.

We are caught up in love for ourselves whenever we give no consideration to our neighbor in what we are thinking and doing, and therefore we give no consideration to the public welfare, let alone the Lord. We are conscious only of ourselves and our immediate circle. This means that when we do something for the sake of ourselves and our immediate circle and it does benefit the public and our neighbor, it is only for the sake of appearances.

In referring to "ourselves and our immediate circle," I mean that when we love ourselves we also love those we claim as our own, specifically our children and grandchildren, and in general everyone with whom we identify, whom we call "ours." Loving them is also loving ourselves. This is because we see them as virtually part of us and see ourselves in them. Included in those we call "ours" is everyone who praises us, respects us, and reveres us.

We are caught up in our love for ourselves when we belittle our neighbors, when we regard anyone who disagrees with us as an enemy—anyone who does not respect and revere us. We are still more deeply caught up in love for ourselves if for such reasons we harbor hatred toward our neighbors and persecute them, and even more deeply if we burn with vengeance toward them and crave their destruction. People who do this eventually come to love cruelty.

We can tell what love for ourselves is like by comparing it to heavenly love. Heavenly love is loving service for its own sake, loving for their own sakes the good things we do for church, country, human community, and fellow citizen. When we love these things for our own sakes, though, we love them only as servants who wait on us. It then follows that when we are caught up in love for ourselves we want our church, country, human communities, and fellow-citizens to serve us rather than wanting to serve them. We place ourselves above them, and them beneath us.

Not only that, but the more deeply we are caught up in heavenly love (which is loving actions that are useful and good and enjoying it when we do them), the more we are led by the Lord, since this is the love in which he is and which comes from him. On the other hand, the more deeply we are caught up in love for ourselves the more we are leading ourselves, and the more we lead ourselves the more we are led by our own individual self, and our own individual self is nothing but evil. That self is in fact the evil that we inherit—which is loving ourselves more than God and the world more than heaven.

Furthermore, to the extent that its reins are loosened (that is, with the removal of the outward restraints exerted by fear of the law and its penalties, and by fear of losing reputation, respect, profit, office, and life), selfish love by its very nature goes so wild that it wants to rule not only over every country on earth but even over heaven and over the Divine itself. It knows no boundary or limit. This is the hidden agenda of all who are caught up in love for themselves, even though it is not evident in the world, where the aforementioned reins and restraints keep it in check. When people like this find themselves blocked, they bide their time until an opportunity occurs.

The result of all this is that when we are caught up in this love we do not realize that this kind of utterly senseless craving lies hidden within us. . . .

LOVE FOR OUR NEIGHBOR, OR GOODWILL

First of all, I need to define "neighbor." After all, this is the one we are called upon to love and the one toward whom we are to extend our goodwill. You see, unless we know what "neighbor" means, we may extend goodwill in basically the same manner indiscriminately—just as much to evil people as to good ones, then, so that our goodwill is not really goodwill. That is, evil people use their generosity to do harm to their neighbor, while good people do good.

Most people nowadays think that everyone is equally their neighbor and that they should be generous to anyone who is in need. It is a matter of Christian prudence, though, to check carefully what a person's life is like and to extend goodwill accordingly. When we are devoted to the inner church we do this discriminatingly and therefore intelligently; but when we are devoted to the outer church we act indiscriminately because we are not capable of making distinctions like this.

The different kinds of neighbor that church people really should be aware of depend on the good that any particular individual is engaged in. Since everything good comes from the Lord, the Lord is our neighbor in the highest sense and to the utmost degree, the neighbor as the source [of all good]. It therefore follows that people are neighbors to us to the extent that they have the Lord in themselves; and since no two people accept the Lord (that is, the good that comes from him) in the same way, no two people are our neighbor in the same way. As to what is good, all the people in the heavens and all good people on earth are different. It never happens that exactly the same goodness is found in any two individuals. The goodness needs to vary so that each kind of goodness can stand on its own.

However, none of us can know all these distinctions and all the consequent distinct kinds of neighbor that arise in accordance with the different ways the Lord is accepted—that is, the way the good from him is accepted. Not even angels can know this except in a general way, by categories and their subcategories; and all the Lord requires of us in the church is that we live by what we know.

Since the goodness in every individual is different, it follows that the nature of each person's goodness determines both the extent to which and the sense in which that individual can function as a neighbor to anyone else. We can see that this is the case from the Lord's parable about the man who fell among thieves, whom both the priest and the Levite passed by, leaving him half dead, while the Samaritan, after he had bound up the man's wounds and poured on oil and wine, lifted him onto his own beast and brought him to the inn and made arrangements for his care. This Samaritan is called "a neighbor" because he put into practice the goodness that is associated with goodwill (Luke 10:29–37). We may know from this that a neighbor is someone who is engaged in doing what is good. The oil and wine that the Samaritan poured into the wounds also mean what is good and the truth that it shows us.

We can see from what has been said thus far that in the broadest sense goodness itself is one's neighbor, since people are neighbors according to the nature of the good that they do, which they get from the Lord. Further, since goodness itself is one's neighbor, love is one's neighbor, because everything good is a matter of love. This means that any individual fulfills the role of a neighbor according to the nature of her or his love, which is the Lord's gift.

It is obvious from people who are mired in love for themselves that love is what makes someone a neighbor and that we are neighbors depending on the nature of our love. Such people recognize as neighbors those who love them the most—that is, those who are most "their own." These they embrace, these they kiss, these they benefit, and these they call kindred. They accept others as neighbors to the extent that they receive love from them, depending therefore on the quality and amount of the love. People like this start with themselves to determine who is their neighbor, because it is their love that makes their neighbor and determines who it is.

People who do not love themselves above all, though (like all who are in the Lord's kingdom), start in determining who their neighbor is with the one whom we ought to love above all—that is, with the Lord—and they accept people as neighbors depending on their love for and from him.

This makes it quite clear where we of the church should start in deciding who our neighbor is, and shows that people are our neighbors depending on the goodness that comes from the Lord—that is, on the basis of goodness in itself.

Furthermore, in Matthew the Lord tells us that this is true:

> He said to the ones who had been engaged in doing good that they had given him something to eat, that they had given him something to drink, welcomed him, clothed him, visited him and come to him in prison, and then said that to the extent that they had done this to one of the least of his family they had done it to him. (Matthew 25:34–40)

These six good deeds, understood spiritually, comprise all the kinds of neighbor.

This also shows that when we love what is good we are loving the Lord, because the Lord is the source of what is good, the one who is devoted to what is good, and the one who is the good itself.

However, it is not just people as individuals who are one's neighbor but people in the plural. That is, it is any smaller or larger community, our country, the church, the Lord's kingdom, and above all the Lord himself. These are "our neighbor," to whom we should do good out of love.

These are also ascending levels of neighbor. A community of many is a neighbor on a higher level than a single individual. On a level still higher is our country, on a level still higher is the church, and on a level still higher is the Lord's kingdom; but on the highest level, our neighbor is the Lord. These ascending levels are like the rungs of a ladder with the Lord at the top.

A community is a neighbor to a greater extent than an individual is because it is made up of many individuals. We are to exercise goodwill toward it just the way we do with respect to individuals, namely, according to the goodness that we find in it. This means that the exercise of goodwill directed toward a community of honest people is totally different from goodwill directed toward a community of dishonest people. We love a community when we are concerned for its welfare because of our love of what is good.

Our country is our neighbor to a greater extent than our community because it is a kind of parent. It is where we were born; it nourishes us and protects us from harm.

We should do good to our country out of love according to its needs, which focus particularly on nourishment for it and on the civil life and the spiritual life of the people who live in it.

If we love our country and do what is good for it because we care about it, then in the other life we love the Lord's kingdom because there the Lord's kingdom is our country. Further, anyone who loves the Lord's kingdom loves the Lord because the Lord is absolutely all there is to his kingdom.

The church is our neighbor to a greater extent than our country because if we care about the church we are caring about the souls and the eternal life of the people of our country. This means that if we care for the church out of love we are loving our neighbor on a higher level because we are longing and striving for heaven and eternal, happy lives for others.

The Lord's kingdom is our neighbor on a still higher level because the Lord's kingdom is made up of all who are engaged in doing what is good, both people on earth and people in the heavens. This means that the Lord's kingdom is where everything that is good is gathered together. When we love this, we love every individual who is engaged in doing what is good.

These are the levels of neighbor, the levels by which love increases for people devoted to love for their neighbor. These levels, though, are in a definite sequence in which the primary or higher is preferable to the secondary or lower; and since the Lord is on the highest level and is to be our central focus on any level as the goal we seek, he is to be loved above all people and all things.

This now enables us to tell how love for the Lord unites itself with love for our neighbor.

It is often said that our neighbor is ourself, meaning that we look after ourselves first. However, a theology of goodwill tells us how we should understand this.

We all need to take care to have the necessities of life, such as the food, clothing, shelter, and more that are necessary for whatever civic life we are involved in. We need to provide these not only for ourselves but also for our dependents, and not only for the present time but also for the future, since unless we acquire the necessities of life for ourselves we cannot be in any condition to extend goodwill. We are in fact in need of everything.

The following comparison may show how we are to be our own neighbors. We all need to provide our bodies with their food and clothing. This needs to come first, but the object is to have a sound mind in a sound body. Furthermore, we all need to provide food for our minds in the form of those things that focus on intelligence and wisdom, the object being that the mind will then be in condition to be of service to our fellow citizens, our human community, our country and church, and therefore the Lord. If we do this we are providing for our well-being to eternity. We can see from this that the main thing is our ultimate purpose in acting, because everything depends on that.

It is also like someone who is building a house. First we need to lay a foundation, but the purpose of the foundation is the house and the purpose of the house is living in it. If we think being a neighbor to ourselves really comes first, it is like regarding the foundation as the objective rather than the house and our life in the house, when in fact our life in the house truly is the first and final goal, and the house and its foundation are only means to this end.

It is the goal that tells how we need to be our own neighbors and look after ourselves first. If the goal is to become richer than others solely for the sake of wealth or for pleasure or eminence or anything like that, it is a bad goal. We are loving ourselves, not our neighbor. If, however, the goal is to acquire wealth in order to be fit to be of service to our fellow citizens, our human community, our country, and our church, this is like seeking office for a like purpose, and we are loving our neighbor.

The actual goal of our actions makes us the people that we are because the goal is our love. For everyone, our first and final goal is what we love above all.

All this is about our neighbor. Now I need to discuss love for our neighbor, or *goodwill.*

Many people believe that love for their neighbor consists of giving to the poor, providing resources to the needy, and doing good to just anyone. Goodwill, though, is acting prudently and with the intent of having a good result. If we provide resources to malefactors who are poor or needy, we are doing harm to our neighbors by providing those resources, because those resources strengthen the malefactors in their evil and supply them with the means of harming others. It is different when we supply resources to good people.

Goodwill, though, reaches out far beyond the poor and needy. Goodwill is doing what is right in everything we do, doing our duty in every position of responsibility. A judge who does what is fair for the sake of fairness is engaged in goodwill. Judges who punish the guilty and acquit the innocent are engaged in goodwill because in doing so they are taking care of their fellow citizens and taking care of their country.

Priests who teach the truth and lead people toward goodness for the sake of what is true and good are engaged in goodwill.

If they do these things for the sake of themselves or for worldly purposes, though, they are not engaged in goodwill, because they are loving themselves rather than their neighbor.

It is the same for others whether they hold some office or not—children toward their parents, for example, and parents toward their children, servants toward their employers and employers toward their servants, subjects toward their monarch and monarchs toward their subjects. If they do their duty for the sake of duty and do what is fair for the sake of fairness, they are engaged in goodwill.

The reason this is a matter of love for our neighbor or goodwill is that everyone is our neighbor, as just noted, but in various ways. A smaller or larger community is more of a neighbor, the country is still more of a neighbor, the Lord's kingdom still more, and the Lord is the neighbor above all. In the broadest sense the goodness that comes from the Lord is our neighbor, which means that what is honest and fair is as well. So people who do anything good because it is good and who do what is honest and fair because it is honest and fair are loving their neighbor and practicing goodwill. This is because their actions are prompted by a love of what is good, honest, and fair and therefore by a love for people in whom we find what is good, honest, and fair.

Goodwill, then, is an inner motivation that makes us want to do what is good and to do this without reward. Doing this is the joy of our life.

When we are doing good from an inner impulse there is goodwill in the very details of what we are thinking and saying, what we are intending and doing. We might say that with respect to our deeper natures, both we and angels are goodwill [itself] when what is good is our neighbor.

This shows how very far goodwill extends.

If people have love for themselves and the world as their goal, there is no way they can be focused on goodwill. They do not even know what goodwill is; and they completely fail to grasp the fact that intending and doing good for their neighbor without looking for payment is a heaven inside them— that inherent in this impulse there is just as much happiness as heaven's angels have: more than words can convey. This is because people who selfishly love themselves and the world believe that if they were deprived of the joy they take in their display of prestige and wealth they would no longer have any joy at all, when in fact that would be the beginning of an infinitely transcendent heavenly joy. . . .

FAITH

No one knows what faith is in its essence who does not know what goodwill is, because where there is no goodwill there is no faith. This is because goodwill is just as inseparable from faith as goodness is from truth. That is, what we love or really care about is what we regard as good, and what we believe in is what we regard as true. We can therefore see that the oneness of goodwill and faith is like the oneness of what is good and what is true.

The oneness of goodwill and faith is also like the oneness of our will and understanding. These are, after all, the two capacities that take in what is good and what is true, our will taking in what is good and our understanding what is true. So, too, these two capacities take in goodwill and faith, because goodness is a matter of goodwill and truth is a matter of faith. No one is ignorant of the fact that goodwill and faith are associated with us and are in us, and since they are associated with us and in us the only place they can exist within us is in our will and our understanding. Our whole life resides there and comes forth from there. We do have memory as well, but that is only a waiting room where things gather that are going to enter our understanding and will. We can see, then, that the oneness of goodwill and faith is like the oneness of will and understanding.

Goodwill unites with faith for us when we will to do what we know and sense. Willing is a matter of goodwill, and knowing and sensing are matters of faith. Faith moves into us and becomes part of us when we both will to do and love what we know and sense. Until that happens, it is outside us.

Faith is not faith for us until it becomes spiritual, and it does not become spiritual unless it becomes a matter of love. It becomes a matter of love when we love to live out what is true and good—that is, to live by what we are commanded in the Word.

Faith consists of being moved by what is true because we want to do what is true simply because it is true; and wanting to do what is true simply because it is true is our actual spiritual nature. That is, it is detached from our earthly nature, which is willing to do what is true not because it is true but for the sake of praise or fame or profit for ourselves. Truth detached from such concerns is spiritual because it comes from the Divine. Whatever comes from the Divine is spiritual, and this is united to us through love because love is spiritual union.

We can know and think and understand a great deal, but when we are left to the privacy of our own thoughts we discard anything that is not in harmony with our love. This means also that we discard such things after our physical lives, when we are in the spirit, since the only things that are left to us once we are in the spirit are the things that have entered into our love. After death all the rest strikes us as foreign matter that we throw out of the house because it is not part of our love. I have said "in the spirit" because we live as spirits after death.

We can form some image of the good that goodwill does and the truth that faith discloses if we think in terms of the warmth and light of the sun. When the light that radiates from the sun is united to warmth, as is the case in spring- and summertime, then everything on earth sprouts and blossoms. When there is no warmth in the light, though, as is the case in wintertime, then everything on earth becomes dormant and dies. Spiritual light is the truth that faith discloses, and spiritual warmth is love.

This enables us to form an image of what people of the church are like when faith is united to goodwill in them. They are just like a garden or park. Their image when faith is not united to goodwill in them is like that of a wasteland and a land buried in snow.

The assurance or trust that is ascribed to faith and is referred to as "truly saving faith" is not a spiritual assurance or trust but an earthly one, if it is a matter of faith alone. Spiritual assurance or trust derives its essence and life from the good that love does but not from the truth that faith discloses apart from that good. The assurance that belongs to faith separated from good is dead, so real assurance is not possible for us when we are leading evil lives. An assurance that we are saved, no matter how we have lived, because of the Lord's merit with the Father does not come from truth either.

Everyone who has spiritual faith has an assurance that we are saved by the Lord. That is, we believe that the Lord came into the world to give eternal life to those who believe and live by the principles that he taught, that he regenerates us and fits us for heaven, and that he does this all by himself without our help, out of pure mercy.

Believing what the Word or the theology of the church teaches and not living by it may look like faith, and some may even believe that they are saved by it; but no one is saved by this alone. This is in fact a *veneer of faith*. It is necessary to describe this veneer of faith at this juncture.

A veneer of faith is when we believe and love the Word and the theology of the church not for the sake of its truth or in order to live by it but for the sake of profit and reputation and for the sake of being considered learned. As a result, when we are devoted to this kind of faith we are not focusing on the Lord or heaven but on ourselves and this world. People who are intensely ambitious and acquisitive in this world are more strongly convinced of the truth of what the church's theology teaches than people who are not intensely ambitious and acquisitive. This is because for them the church's theology is nothing but a means to their own ends, and the more they love those ends, the more they love—and trust—the means.

Essentially, though, the fact is that they are caught up in this conviction to the extent that they are on fire with their love for themselves and the world and are speaking and preaching and acting from that fire. At such times they are completely convinced that what they are saying is true. However, when they are not caught up in the fire of those loves they believe very little—some do not believe at all. This shows that a veneer of faith is a faith of the lips and not of the heart, so it is really no faith at all.

People whose faith is just a veneer do not know from any inner enlightenment whether what they are teaching is true or false, and as long as average people believe them, they do not care. In fact, they are not moved in the least by truth for its own sake. As a result, if they cannot obtain status or profit they abandon their faith (or at least if they can do so without putting their reputation in jeopardy), because the veneer of faith does not dwell inside us. Rather, it stands outside, in our memory alone, so we can call on it when we are teaching. This means that this faith and its truths vanish after death because the only elements of faith that remain then are the ones that have a place inside us—that is, the elements of faith that have taken root in doing what is good, and that have therefore been made part of our life.

The following passage in Matthew is about people whose faith is just a veneer:

> Many will say to me in that day, "Lord, Lord, haven't we prophesied in your name and cast out demons in your name and done many worthwhile things in your name?" But then I will declare to them, "I do not recognize you, workers of iniquity." (Matthew 7:22–23)

Then it says in Luke:

> Then you will begin to say, "We have eaten with you and drunk, and you have taught in our streets." But he will say, "I tell you, I do not know where you come from. Go away from me, all you workers of iniquity." (Luke 13:26–27)

They are also described as the five foolish young women in Matthew who did not have oil for their lamps:

> Finally those young women arrived, saying, "Lord, lord, open up for us." But he will say in response, "I tell you in truth, I do not recognize you." (Matthew 25:11–12)

[In the Word,] oil in lamps symbolizes the good that love does in faith.

FREEDOM

All freedom is a matter of love, because what we love we do freely. That is also why all freedom is a matter of will, because whatever we love we also will to do; and since love and will constitute our life, freedom also constitutes it. This can show us what freedom is, namely, that it is whatever belongs to our love and will and therefore to our life. That is why anything we do freely seems to us to have come from ourselves.

Doing evil freely seems to be freedom but it is slavery, since this freedom comes from our love for ourselves and our love for the world, and these loves come from hell. This kind of freedom actually turns into slavery after we die, too, since anyone who had this kind of freedom becomes a worthless slave in hell afterwards.

In contrast, freely doing what is good is freedom itself because it comes from a love for the Lord and from a love for our neighbor, and these loves come from heaven. This freedom too stays with us after death and then becomes true freedom because anyone who has this kind of freedom is like one of the family in heaven. The Lord says it like this: "Everyone who commits sin is a slave of sin. A slave does not stay in the house forever. A son or daughter does stay forever. If the Son has made you free, you will be truly free" (John 8:34–36).

Since everything good comes from the Lord and everything evil from hell, then it follows that freedom is being led by the Lord and slavery is being led by hell.

The purpose of our having a freedom to think and do what is evil or false (to the extent that the law does not prevent it) is that we can be reformed. That is, what is good and what is true need to be planted in our love and will if they are to become part of our life, and there is no way this can happen unless we have the freedom to contemplate what is evil and false as well as what is good and true. This freedom is given to each one of us by the Lord; and when we are contemplating something that is good and true, then to the extent that we do not at the same time love what is evil and false the Lord plants goodness and truth in our love and will and therefore in our life, and in this way reforms us.

Anything that is sown in freedom also lasts, while anything sown in compulsion does not last. This is because anything we are compelled to do does not come from our own will but rather from the will of the one who is compelling us.

That is also why worship from freedom is pleasing to the Lord but compulsory worship is not. That is, worship from freedom is worship from love, while compulsory worship is not.

No matter how similar they look on the surface, freedom to do good and freedom to do evil are as different and as remote from each other as heaven and hell. Then too, the freedom to do good comes from heaven and is called "heavenly freedom," while the freedom to do evil comes from hell and is called "hellish freedom." To the extent that we have the one freedom we do not have the other—no one, that is, can serve two masters (Matthew 6:24). We can also see from this that people who have hellish freedom think that it is slavery and compulsion if they are not allowed to will what is evil and think what is false whenever they feel like it, while people who have heavenly freedom loathe to will anything evil and to think anything false, and if they are forced to do so, it torments them.

Since acting from freedom seems to us to come from ourselves, heavenly freedom can also be called "heavenly selfhood" and hellish freedom can be called "hellish selfhood." Hellish selfhood is the sense of self into which we are born, and it is evil. Heavenly selfhood, though, is the selfhood into which we are reformed, and it is good.

This shows us what *freedom of choice* is—namely, that it is doing what is good by choice or intentionally, and that we have this freedom when we are being led by the Lord. We are led by the Lord when we love what is good and true because it is good and true.

We can tell what kind of freedom we have from the pleasure we feel when we think, speak, act, hear, and see, because all pleasure is an effect of love.

# REPENTANCE

Now that faith, goodwill, and free choice have been treated, the related topic of repentance comes next, because without repentance there can be no true faith and no genuine goodwill, and no one could repent without free choice. Another reason why there is a treatment of repentance at this point is that the topic that follows is regeneration, and none of us can be regenerated before the more serious evils that make us detestable before God have been removed; repentance is what removes them.

What else are unregenerate people but impenitent? And what else are impenitent people but those who are in a drowsy state of apathy? They know nothing about sin and therefore cherish it deep within themselves and make love to it every day the way an adulterous man makes love to a promiscuous woman who shares his bed.

To make known what repentance is and what effect it has, this treatment of it will be divided into separate headings.

REPENTANCE IS THE BEGINNING OF THE CHURCH WITHIN US

The extended community that is known as the church consists of all the people who have the church within them. The church takes hold in us when we are regenerated, and we are all regenerated when we abstain from things that are evil and sinful and run away from them as we would run if we saw hordes of hellish spirits pursuing us with flaming torches, intending to attack us and throw us onto a bonfire.

As we go through the early stages of our lives, there are many things that prepare us for the church and introduce us into it; but acts of repentance are the things that actually produce the church within us. Acts of repentance include any and all actions that result in our not willing, and consequently not doing, evil things that are sins against God.

Before repentance, we stand outside regeneration. In that condition, if any thought of eternal salvation somehow makes its way into us, we at first turn toward it but soon turn away. That thought does not penetrate us any farther than the outer areas where we have ideas; it then goes out into our spoken words and perhaps into a few gestures that go along with those words. When the thought of eternal salvation penetrates our will, however, then it is truly inside us. The will is the real self, because it is where our love dwells; our thoughts are outside us, unless they come from our will, in which case our will and our thought act as one, and together make us who we are. From these points it follows that in order for repentance to be genuine and effective within us, it has to be done both by our will and by thinking that comes from our will. It cannot be done by thought alone. Therefore it has to be a matter of actions, and not of words alone.

The Word makes it obvious that repentance is the beginning of the church. John the Baptist was sent out in advance to prepare people for the church that the Lord was about to establish. At the same time as he was baptizing people he was also preaching repentance; his baptism was therefore called a baptism of repentance. Baptism means a spiritual washing, that is, being cleansed from sins. John baptized in the Jordan River because the Jordan means introduction into the church, since it was the first border of the land of Canaan, where the church was. The Lord himself also preached that people should repent so that their sins would be forgiven. He taught, in effect, that repentance is the beginning of the church; that if we repent, the sins within us will be removed; and that if our sins are removed, they are also forgiven. Furthermore, when the Lord sent out his twelve apostles and also the seventy, he commanded them to preach repentance. From all this it is clear that repentance is the beginning of the church.

It can also be illustrated through the following comparisons. No one can pasture flocks of sheep, goats, and lambs in fields or woodlands that are already occupied by all kinds of predatory animals, without first driving away the predators. No one can turn land that is full of thorny bushes, brambles, and stinging nettles into a garden without first uprooting those harmful plants. No one can go into a city that is occupied by hostile enemy forces, set up a new administration devoted to justice and judgment, and make it a good place for citizens to live without first expelling the enemy. It is similar with the evils that are inside us. They are like predatory animals, brambles and thorny bushes, and enemies. The church could no more live alongside them than we could live in a cage full of tigers and leopards; or lie down in a bed whose sheets were lined, and pillows stuffed, with poisonous plants; or sleep at night in a church building under whose stone floor there are tombs with dead bodies in them—would we not be harassed there by ghosts that were like the Furies? . . .

WE MUST LAY OUR EVILS ASIDE THROUGH REPENTANCE

We are all born with a tendency toward evils. As is recognized in the church, from our mother's womb we are nothing but evil. Now, the reason this is recognized is that the church councils and leaders have passed down to us the notion that Adam's sin has been passed on to all his descendants; in this view, this is the sole reason why Adam and everyone since has been condemned; and this damnation clings to us all from the day we are born. Many teachings of the church are based on these assertions. For example, [we are told that] the Lord instituted the washing of regeneration that is called baptism so that this sin would be removed. This sin was also the reason for the Lord's Coming. Faith in his merit is the means by which this sin is removed. The churches have many other teachings as well that are based on this notion. . . .

My friend, the evil we inherit comes in fact from no other source than our own parents. What we inherit, though, is not evil that we ourselves actually commit but an inclination toward evil. . . . We may have a greater or a lesser tendency to a specific evil. Therefore after death no one is judged on the basis of his or her inherited evil; we are judged only on the basis of our actual evils, the evils we ourselves have committed. This is clear from the following commandment of the Lord: "Parents will not be put to death for their children; children will not be put to death for their parents. Each will die for her or his own sins" (Deuteronomy 24:16). I have become certain of this from my experience in the spiritual world of little children who had died. They have an inclination toward evils and will them, but they do not do them, because they are brought up under the Lord's supervision and are saved.

The only thing that breaks the inclination and tendency toward evil that is passed on by parents to their offspring and descendants is the new birth from the Lord that is called regeneration. In the absence of rebirth, this inclination not only remains uninterrupted but even grows from one generation to the next and becomes a stronger tendency toward evil until it encompasses evils of every kind. . . .

From what has gone before, it is evident that no evil can be laid aside except by the Lord, working in those who believe in him and who love their neighbor. The Lord, goodwill, and faith form a unity in the same way our life, our will, and our understanding form a unity; if we separate them, each one crumbles like a pearl that is crushed to powder. How can we become part of that unity? We cannot unless we lay aside at least some of our evils through repentance. I say that *we* lay aside our evils, because the Lord does not lay them aside by himself without our cooperation.

There is a saying that no one can fulfill the law, especially since someone who breaks one of the Ten Commandments breaks them all [James 2:10–11; Matthew 5:19]. But this formulaic saying does not mean what it seems to. The proper way to understand it is that people who purposely or deliberately behave in a way that is contrary to one commandment in effect behave contrary to the rest, because doing something [against one commandment] purposely and deliberately is the same as completely denying that that behavior is sinful and rejecting any argument to the contrary. And people who thus deny and reject the very idea of sin do not care whether *any* given act is labeled a sin or not.

This is the type of resolve developed by people who do not want to hear anything about repentance. People who, through repentance, have laid aside some evils that are sins, though, develop a resolve to believe in the Lord and to love their neighbor. They are held by the Lord in a resolution to abstain from many other things as well. Therefore if it happens that because they did not realize what was going on or because they were overwhelmed by desire, they commit a sin, it is not held against them. It was not something they had planned to do, and they do not support what they did.

I may reinforce this point as follows. In the spiritual world I have come across many people who had shared a similar lifestyle when they were in the physical world. They all dressed in fashionable clothing, enjoyed fine dining, took profit from their business, went to the theater, told jokes about lovers as if they themselves were lustful, and many other things of the kind. Yet for some of these people the angels labeled their behaviors as evil and sinful, whereas for others the angels did not. The angels declared the former guilty and the latter innocent. Upon being asked why this was, since the people had done the same things, the angels replied that they had evaluated all the people on the basis of their plans, intentions, and purposes and distinguished them accordingly. Those whose intent excused them, the angels excused, and those whose intent condemned them, the angels condemned, since all who are in heaven have good intent, and all who are in hell have evil intent.

These points may be illustrated with comparisons. The sins that we retain when we do not practice repentance are like various diseases we suffer that are fatal unless we are given medicine that takes away what is causing harm. Such sins are especially like gangrene, which spreads (if not caught in time) and inevitably leads to death. They are like boils and abscesses that have not been lanced and opened—the accumulation of pus will press into surrounding tissues, then into nearby internal organs, and finally into the heart, causing death. . . .

As experienced gardeners know, a trunk that comes from bad seed or a bad root sends its noxious sap into the branch of a good tree that has been grafted onto it, and the bad sap that creeps up that branch is then turned into good sap and produces useful fruit. Something similar occurs in us when evil is laid aside through the process of repentance; through repentance we are grafted onto the Lord like a branch onto a vine and we bear good fruit (John 15:4, 5, 6).

REPENTANCE BEGINS WHEN WE LOOK FOR SIN IN OURSELVES

It is impossible for anyone in the Christian world to lack a concept of sin. Everyone in Christianity from early childhood on is taught what evil is, and from youth on is taught which evils are sinful. . . . The evil that is sinful is simply evil against our neighbor; and evil against our neighbor is also evil against God, which is what sin is.

Nevertheless, having a concept of sin does nothing for us unless we examine the actions we have taken in our lives and see whether we have either openly or secretly done any such thing.

Before we take this action, everything about sin is just an idea to us; what the preacher says about it is only a sound that comes in our left ear, goes out our right ear, and is gone. Eventually it becomes a subject relegated to vague thoughts and mumbled words in worship, and for many it comes to seem like something imaginary and mythical.

Something completely different occurs, however, if we examine ourselves in the light of our concepts of what is sinful, discover some such thing in ourselves, say to ourselves, "This evil is sinful," and then abstain from it out of fear of eternal punishment. Then for the first time we receive the instructive and eloquent preaching in church in *both* of our ears, take it to heart, and turn from a non-Christian into a Christian.

What could possibly be better known across the entire Christian world than the idea that we should examine ourselves? Everywhere in both Roman Catholic and Protestant empires and monarchies, as people approach the Holy Supper they are given teachings and warnings that they must examine themselves, recognize and admit to their sins, and start a new life of a different nature. In British territories this is done with terrifying threats. During the prayer that precedes communion, the priest by the altar reads and proclaims the following:

> The way and means of becoming a worthy partaker in the Holy Supper is first to examine your life and your conversations by the rule of God's commandments. In whatever regard you notice that you have committed an offense of will, speech, or act, then bewail your own sinfulness and confess yourselves to Almighty God, with full purpose of amending your life. If you observe that your offenses are not only against God but

also against your neighbors, you shall reconcile your-selves to them, being ready to make restitution and sat-isfaction to the utmost of your power for all injuries and wrongs done by you to any other, and being like-wise ready to forgive others who have offended you, just as you wish to have forgiveness from God for your offenses. Otherwise receiving the Holy Supper does nothing but increase your damnation. Therefore if any of you is a blasphemer of God, or a hinderer or slan-derer of his Word, or an adulterer, or someone taken with malice or ill will, or involved in any other grievous crime, repent of your sins. Or else do not come to the Holy Supper; otherwise, after you take it the Devil may enter into you as he entered into Judas, fill you with all wickedness, and bring you to destruction of both body and soul.

Nevertheless, there are some people who are incapable of examining themselves: for example, children and young men and women before they reach the age at which they can reflect upon themselves; simple people who lack the ability to reflect; all who have no fear of God; some who have a mental or phys-ical illness; and also people who, entrenched in the teaching that justification comes solely through the faith that assigns us Christ's merit, have convinced themselves that if they practiced self-examination and repentance something of their own selves might intrude that would ruin their faith and divert or redirect their salvation from its sole focus.

For the types of people just listed, an oral confession is of benefit, although it is not the same as practicing repentance.

People who know what sin is and especially those who know a lot about it from the Word and who teach about it, but who do not examine themselves and therefore see no sin within themselves, can be compared to people who scrape and save money, only to put it away in boxes and containers and make no other use of it than looking at it and counting it. They are like people who collect pieces of gold and silver jewelry and keep them in a safe in a storage room for no other purpose than to own them. . . .

ACTIVE REPENTANCE

. . . From [teachings in the Bible] it is clear that we absolutely have to repent. What repentance involves, however, and how we go about it will be shown in what follows.

With the reasoning powers we have been given, surely we are all able to understand that repentance does not consist of a mere oral confession that we are a sinner and of listing a number of things about sin, like a hypocrite. What is easier for us, when we feel anguish and agony, than breathing out and emitting sighs and groans through our lips, beating our chests, and declaring ourselves guilty of sins of every kind, even if we are actually unaware of a single sin within ourselves? Does the Devil's gang, which lives inside our loves, go out of us along with our sighing? Surely they whistle contemptuously at our histrionics, and stay inside us as before, since we are their home.

These points serve to clarify that by "repentance" the Word does not mean mere confession; as I said before, it means a repentance from evil actions.

The question then is, How are we to repent? The answer is, we are to do so *actively*. That is, we are to examine ourselves, recognize and admit to our sins, pray to the Lord, and begin a new life.

The fact that repentance is not possible without examining ourselves was shown under the previous heading. And what is the point of examining ourselves unless we recognize our sins? What is the point of that recognition unless we admit that those sins are in us? What is the point of all three of these steps unless we confess our sins before the Lord, pray for his help, and then begin a new life, which is the purpose of the whole exercise? This is active repentance.

The fact that this is the sequence of actions to take is something we are all capable of realizing as we leave childhood and become more and more independent and able to reason for ourselves. We can see this from thinking of our baptism. The washing of baptism means regeneration; and during the ceremony our godparents promised on our behalf that we were going to reject the Devil and all his works. Likewise thinking of the Holy Supper, we have all been warned that in order to approach it worthily we have to repent from our sins, turn ourselves to God, and start a new life. We can also think of the Ten Commandments—the catechism that is in the hands of all Christians. Six of the ten simply command us not to do evil things. If we do not remove these evils through repentance, we are unable to love our neighbor and even less able to love God, even though the Law and the Prophets, that is, the Word and therefore salvation, hinge on these two commandments [Matthew 22:40].

Repentance becomes effective if we practice it regularly— that is, every time we prepare ourselves to take the Communion of the Holy Supper. Afterward, if we abstain from one sin or another that we have discovered in ourselves, this is enough to make our repentance real. When we reach this point, we are on the pathway to heaven, because we then begin to turn from an earthly person into a spiritual person and to be born anew with the help of the Lord.

This change can be illustrated by the following comparison. Before repentance, we are like a desert, inhabited by terrifying wild creatures, dragons, eagle-owls, screech owls, vipers, and bloodletting snakes; in the clumps of bushes in that desert there are the owls and vultures [mentioned in the Bible], and satyrs are dancing [Isaiah 13:21]. After these creatures have been expelled by human work and effort, however, that desert can be plowed and cultivated into fields, and these can be planted with oats, beans, and flax, and later on with barley and wheat.

This can also be compared to the wickedness that is abundant and dominant in humankind. If evildoers were not chastised and punished with whippings and death, no city would survive; no nation would last. In effect, each one of us is society itself in its smallest form. If we do not treat ourselves in a spiritual way as evildoers are treated by the larger society in an earthly way, we are going to be chastised and punished after death; and this will continue until out of sheer fear of further punishment we stop doing evil, even if we can never be compelled to do what is good out of love for it.

TRUE REPENTANCE IS EXAMINING NOT ONLY OUR ACTIONS BUT OUR INTENTIONS

The reason why true repentance is to examine not only the actions of our life but also the intentions of our will is that our understanding and our will produce our actions. We speak from our thought and we act from our will; therefore our speech is our thought speaking, and our action is our will acting. Since this is the origin of what we say and do, it is clear without a doubt that it is these two faculties that commit the sin when our body sins.

It is in fact possible for us to repent of evil things we have done through our bodies but still think about evil and will it. This is like cutting down the trunk of a bad type of tree but leaving its root still in the ground; the same bad tree grows up from the root again and also spreads itself around. There is a different outcome when the root is pulled up, though; and this is what happens within us when we explore the intentions of our will and lay our evils aside through repentance.

We explore the intentions of our will by exploring our thoughts. Our intentions reveal themselves in our thoughts— for example, when we contemplate, will, and intend acts of revenge, adultery, theft, or false witness, or entertain desires for those things. This applies as well to acts of blasphemy against God, against the holy Word, and against the church, and so on.

If we keep our minds focused on these issues, and explore whether we would do such things if no fear of the law or concern for our reputation stood in the way, and if after this exploration we decide that we do not will those things, because they are sins, then we are practicing a repentance that is true and deep. This is even more the case when we are feeling delight in those evils and are free to do them, but at that moment we resist and abstain. If we practice this over and over, then when our evils come back we sense our delight in them as something unpleasant, and in time we condemn them to hell. This is the meaning of these words of the Lord: "Any who try to find their soul will lose it, and any who lose their soul for my sake, will find it" (Matthew 10:39).

People who remove evils from their will through this type of repentance are like those who in time pulled up the weeds that had been sown by the Devil in their field, allowing seeds planted by the Lord God the Savior to gain free ground and to sprout for the harvest (Matthew 13:25–30).

There are two loves that have been deeply rooted in the human race for a long time now: love for dominating everyone, and love for possessing everyone's wealth. If the reins are let out on the first type of love, it rushes on until it wants to be the God of all heaven. If the reins are let out on the second type of love, it rushes on until it wants to be the God of the whole world. All other forms of love for evil are ranked below these two and serve as their army.

These two loves are extremely difficult to find by self-examination. They live at a deep level within us and hide themselves away. They are like vipers lurking in a craggy rock surface that save up their venom so that when someone falls asleep on the rock, they strike lethal blows and then slither back out of sight.

These loves are also like the sirens mentioned by ancient writers. The sirens would use their singing to lure people in and kill them.

These two loves dress themselves up in robes and tunics just the way devils use magic to project images in order to appear well dressed before their own cronies and others they wish to deceive.

It is important to note, however, that these two loves can be more prevalent among commoners than among the great; more prevalent among the poor than among the wealthy; more prevalent among subjects than among royalty. The latter in each case are born into power and wealth. Over time, the latter come to view their power and wealth much the way people at a somewhat lower level—commanders, governors, admirals, or even impoverished farm workers—view their own households and possessions. It is not the same, though, when monarchs wish to exercise power over nations that are not their own.

The intentions of our will must be examined, because our love resides in our will. Our will is a vessel for our love. From its residence in our will, our whole love imparts its feelings of delight to the perceptions and thoughts in our understanding. Our perceptions and thoughts do nothing on their own; they serve our will. They are in harmony with our will and agree with and support everything that has to do with our love.

Our will, then, is the home in which we live. Our understanding is just the front hall through which we go in and out. This is why I said above that we must examine the intentions of our will. When these are examined and have been laid aside, we are lifted from our earthly will—where the evils we inherited and the evils we have actually committed are lodged—to our spiritual will. Through that higher will, the Lord reforms and regenerates our earthly will, and also works through it to reform and regenerate the sensory and voluntary faculties of our body, until the process has encompassed the whole of us.

People who do not examine themselves are like people with a sickness that closes off their capillaries and therefore corrupts their blood, causing their limbs to go to sleep and atrophy, and resulting in severe chronic diseases because their humors, and therefore the blood that arises from them, are viscous, sticky, irritating, and acidic. People who do examine themselves, however, including the intentions of their will, are like people who are healed from these diseases and regain the vitality they felt when they were young.

People who examine themselves in the right way are like ships from Ophir completely filled with gold, silver, and precious stones; before they examined themselves, though, they were like barges loaded down with unclean freight, carting away the filth and excrement from city streets. . . .

DOING GOOD AS RELIGIOUS PRACTICE

In the Protestant Christian world, active repentance, which is examining ourselves, recognizing and admitting to our sins, praying to the Lord, and starting a new life, is extremely difficult to practice, for a number of reasons that will be covered later. Therefore here is an easier kind of repentance: When we are considering doing something evil and are forming an intention to do it, we say to ourselves, "I am thinking about this and I am intending to do it, but because it is a sin, I am not going to do it." This counteracts the enticement that hell is injecting into us and keeps it from making further inroads.

It is amazing but true that it is easy for any of us to rebuke someone else who is intending to do something evil and say, "Don't do that—that's a sin!" And yet it is difficult for us to say the same thing to ourselves. The reason is that saying it to ourselves requires a movement of the will, but saying it to someone else requires only a low level of thought based on things we have heard.

There was an investigation in the spiritual world to see which people were capable of doing this second type of repentance. It was discovered that there are as few of such people as there are doves in a vast desert. Some people indicated that they were indeed capable of this second type of repentance, but that they were incapable of examining themselves and confessing their sins before God. Nevertheless, all people who do good actions as a religious practice avoid actual evils. It is extremely rare, though, that people reflect on the inner realms that belong to their will. They suppose that because they are involved in good actions they are not involved in evil actions, and even that their goodness covers up their evil.

But, my friend, to abstain from evils is the first step in gaining goodwill. The Word teaches this. The Ten Commandments teach it. Baptism teaches it. The Holy Supper teaches it.

Reason, too, teaches it. How could any of us escape from our evils or drive them away without ever taking a look at ourselves? How can our goodness become truly good without being inwardly purified?

I know that all devout people and also all people of sound reason who read this will nod and see it as genuine truth; yet even so, only a few are going to do what it says.

Nevertheless, all people who do what is good as a religious practice—not only Christians but also non-Christians—are accepted and adopted by the Lord after they die. The Lord says, "'I was hungry and you gave me something to eat. I was thirsty and you gave me something to drink. I was a stranger and you took me in. I was naked and you clothed me. I was sick and you visited me. I was in prison and you came to me.' And he said, 'As much as you did this to one of the least of my people, you did it to me. Come, you who are blessed, and possess as your inheritance the kingdom prepared for you from the foundation of the world'" (Matthew 25:34–36, 40). . . .

It is important to realize that people who do what is good only because they possess a natural goodness and not because of their religion are not accepted [by the Lord] after they die. This is because the only goodness that was in their goodwill was earthly and not also spiritual; and spiritual goodness is what forges a partnership between the Lord and us, not earthly goodness without spiritual goodness. Earthly goodness is of the flesh alone, and is inherited at our birth from our parents. Spiritual goodness is goodness of the spirit and is born anew with the help of the Lord.

People who, as a religious practice, do good actions that have to do with goodwill and, as part of that same practice, do not do evil things, but who have not yet accepted the teaching of the new church about the Lord, can be compared to trees that bear good fruit, but only a few pieces of it. Such people are also like trees that bear pieces of fruit that are fine but small; the trees are nevertheless kept and taken care of in gardens. They can also be compared to olive trees and fig trees that grow wild in the forest, and to fragrant herbs and balsam bushes that grow wild on hills. They are like little buildings that are houses of God in which devout worship occurs. They are the sheep on the right [Matthew 25:33], and are examples of the ram that was attacked by a goat in Daniel 8:2–14. In heaven their clothes are red. After they have been initiated into the good actions and attitudes taught by the new church, however, their clothes become purple and (if they also accept the truths of the new church) more and more beautifully radiant.

WE NEED TO ASK THE LORD FOR HELP

It is the Lord God the Savior to whom we must turn, (1) because he is the God of heaven and earth, the Redeemer and Savior, who has omnipotence, omniscience, and omnipresence, who is both mercy and justice itself, and (2) because we are his creation and the church is his sheepfold, and we are commanded many times in the New Covenant to turn to him and worship and adore him.

In the following words in John the Lord commands that we are to turn to him alone:

Truly, truly I say to you, those who do not enter through the door to the sheepfold but instead climb up some other way are thieves and robbers. The person who goes in through the door is the shepherd of the sheep. I am the door. Anyone who enters through me will be saved and will find pasture. The thief does not come except to steal, slaughter, and destroy. I have come so that they may have life and abundance. I am the good shepherd. (John 10:1, 2, 9, 10, 11)

The "other way" that we are not to climb up is toward God the Father, because he cannot be seen, and is therefore inaccessible and unavailable for partnership. This is why he came into the world and made himself able to be seen, accessible, and available for partnership. He did this for only one reason: so that human beings could be saved. If we do not direct our thinking toward God *as a human being,* our whole mental sight of God is lost. It collapses like our eyesight when we send it out into the universe. Instead of God we see empty nothingness, or nature as a whole, or certain objects within nature.

The being who came into the world was God himself, who from eternity [has been and] is the One. This is very clear from the birth of the Lord and Savior. He was conceived by the power of the Highest through the Holy Spirit. As a result the Virgin Mary gave birth to his human manifestation. It follows then that his soul was the Divinity itself that is called the Father—God is, after all, indivisible—and the human being born as a result is the human manifestation of God the Father, which is called the Son of God (Luke 1:32, 34, 35). It follows from all this that when we turn to the Lord God the Savior, we are turning to God the Father as well. This is why he replied to Philip, when Philip asked him to show them the Father, "Those who see me see the Father. How then can you say, 'Show us the Father'? Do you not believe that I am in the Father and the

Father is in me? Believe me that I am in the Father and the Father is in me" (John 14:6–11).

There are two duties that we are obliged to perform after we have examined ourselves: prayer and confession. The *prayer* is to be a request that [the Lord] have mercy on us, give us the power to resist the evils that we have repented of, and provide us an inclination and desire to do what is good, since "without him we cannot do anything" (John 15:5). The *confession* is to be that we see, recognize, and admit to our evils and that we are discovering that we are miserable sinners.

There is no need for us to list our sins before the Lord and no need to beg that he forgive them. The reason we do not need to list our sins before the Lord is that we searched them out within ourselves and saw them, and therefore they are present before the Lord because they are present before us. The Lord was leading us in our self-examination; he disclosed our sins; he inspired our grief and, along with it, the motivation to stop doing them and to begin a new life.

There are two reasons why we should not beg the Lord to forgive our sins. The first is that sins are not abolished, they are just relocated within us. They are laid aside when after repentance we stop doing them and start a new life. This is because there are countless yearnings that stick to each evil in a kind of cluster; these cannot be set aside in a moment, but they can be dealt with in stages as we allow ourselves to be reformed and regenerated.

The second reason is that the Lord is mercy itself. Therefore he forgives the sins of all people. He blames no one for any sin. He says, "They do not know what they are doing" [Luke 23:34] (but this does not mean our sins are taken away altogether). To Peter, who was asking how many times he should forgive a friend who was sinning against him—whether he should give forgiveness as many as seven times—the Lord answered, "I do not say as many as seven times, but as many as seventy times seven" (Matthew 18:21, 22). How forgiving, then, is the Lord?

It does no harm, though, for people who are weighed down by a heavy conscience to lighten their load by listing their sins before a minister of the church, for the sake of absolution. Doing so introduces them to the habit of examining themselves and reflecting on their daily evils. Nevertheless, this type of confession is earthly in nature, whereas the confession described above is spiritual.

Giving adoration to some vicar [of Christ] on earth as we would to God or calling on some saint as we would call on God has no more effect on heaven than worshiping the sun, the moon, and the stars, or seeking for a response from fortune-tellers and believing in their meaningless utterances. Doing this would be like worshiping a church building but not God, who is in that church. It would be like submitting a request for glorious honors not to the king himself but to a servant of the king who is carrying his scepter and crown. This would be pointless, like paying deference to a gleaming scarlet robe but not the person who is wearing it; like praising the glorious light and golden rays from the sun but not the sun itself; like saluting names but not people. The following statement in John is for people who do such things: "We must remain in truth in Jesus Christ. He is the true God and eternal life. Little children, beware of idols" (1 John 5:20, 21).

REPENTANCE IS EASY FOR THOSE WHO PRACTICE IT

Active repentance is examining ourselves, recognizing [and admitting to] our sins, confessing them before the Lord, and beginning a new life. This accords with the description of it under the preceding headings. People in the Protestant Christian world—by which I here mean all [Christians] who have separated from the Roman Catholic Church, and also people who belong to that church but have not practiced active repentance—experience tremendous inner resistance to such repentance, for various reasons. Some do not want to do it. Some are afraid. They are in the habit of not doing it, and this breeds first unwillingness, and then intellectual and rational support for not doing it, and in some cases, grief, dread, and terror of it. . . .

It is well known that habits form a kind of second nature, and therefore what is easy for one person is difficult for another. This applies also to examining ourselves and confessing what we have found.

It is easy for manual laborers, porters, and farm workers to work with their arms from morning till evening, but a delicate person of the nobility cannot do the same work for half an hour without fatigue and sweating. It is easy for a forerunner with a walking stick and comfortable shoes to ply the road for miles, whereas someone used to riding in a carriage has difficulty jogging slowly from one street to the next. All artisans who are devoted to their craft pursue it easily and willingly, and when they are away from it they long to get back to it; but it is almost impossible to force a lazy person with the same skills to practice that craft. The same goes for everyone who has some occupation or pursuit.

What is easier for someone who is pursuing religious devotion than praying to God? And what is more difficult for someone who is enslaved to ungodliness?

All priests are afraid the first time they preach before royalty. But after they get used to it, they go on boldly.

What is easier for angelic people than lifting their eyes up to heaven? What is easier for devilish people than casting their eyes down to hell? (If they are hypocrites, however, they can look toward heaven in a similar way, but with aversion of heart.)

We are all saturated with the goal we have in mind and the habits that result from it.

THOSE WHO HAVE NEVER PRACTICED REPENTANCE DO NOT KNOW WHAT GOOD AND EVIL ARE

Since only a few people in the Protestant Christian world practice repentance, it is important to add that those who have not looked at or studied themselves eventually do not even know what damnable evil or saving goodness is, because they lack the religious practice that would allow them to find out. The evil that we do not see, recognize, or admit to stays with us; and what stays with us becomes more and more firmly established until it blocks off the inner areas of our minds. As a result, we become first earthly, then sense-oriented, and finally bodily. In these cases we do not know of any damnable evil or any saving goodness. We become like a tree on a hard rock that spreads its roots into the crevices in the rocks and eventually dries up because it has no moisture.

All people who were brought up properly are rational and moral. There are different ways of being rational, however: a worldly way and a heavenly way. People who have become rational and moral in a worldly way but not also in a heavenly way are rational and moral only in word and gesture. Inwardly they are animals, and predatory animals at that, because they are in step with the inhabitants of hell, all of whom are like that. People who have become rational and moral in a heavenly way as well, however, are truly rational and truly moral, because they have these qualities in spirit as well as in word and deed. Something spiritual lies hidden within their words and actions like the soul that activates their earthly, sense-oriented, and bodily levels. Such people are in step with the inhabitants of heaven.

Therefore there is such a thing as a rational, moral person who is spiritual, and such a thing as a rational, moral person who is only earthly. In the world you cannot tell them apart, especially if their hypocrisy is well rehearsed. Angels in heaven can tell the two apart, however, as easily as telling doves from eagle-owls or sheep from tigers.

Those who are only earthly can see good and evil qualities in others and criticize them, but because they have never looked at or studied themselves, they see no evil in themselves. If someone else discovers an evil in them, they use their rational faculty to hide it, as a snake hides its head in the dust; then they plunge themselves into that evil the way a hornet dives into dung.

Their delight in evil is what has this blinding effect. It surrounds them like a fog over a swamp, absorbing and suffocating rays of light. This is the nature of hellish delight. It radiates from hell and flows into every human being, but only into the soles of our feet, our back, and the back of our head. If we receive that inflow with our forehead and our chest, however, we are slaves to hell, because the human cerebrum serves the understanding and its wisdom, whereas the cerebellum serves the will and its love. This is why we have two brains. The only thing that can amend, reform, and turn around hellish delight of the kind just mentioned is a rationality and morality that is spiritual.

Allow me to briefly describe people whose rationality and morality are merely earthly. Such people are truly sense-oriented. If they continue in this direction, they become bodily or carnal. The description that follows will be presented as a list of points in outline form.

"Sensory" is a term for the lowest level of life within the human mind; it clings, and is closely joined, to the five senses of the human body.

"Sense-oriented people" are people who judge everything on the basis of their physical senses—people who will not believe anything unless they can see it with their eyes and touch it with their hands. What they can see and touch they call "something." Everything else they reject.

The inner levels of their mind, levels that see in heaven's light, are closed to the point where they see nothing true related to heaven or the church. Their thinking occurs on an outermost level and not inside, where the light is spiritual. Since the light they have is dull and earthly, people like this are inwardly opposed to things related to heaven and the church, although they are outwardly able to speak in favor of them. If they have hope of gaining ruling power or wealth by so doing, they are even capable of speaking ardently in favor of them.

The educated and the scholarly who are deeply convinced of falsities—especially people who oppose the truths in the Word—are more sense-oriented than others.

Sense-oriented people are able to reason sharply and skillfully, because their thinking is so close to their speech as to be practically in it—almost inside their lips; and also because they attribute all intelligence solely to the ability to speak from memory. They also have great skill at defending things that are false. After they have defended falsities convincingly, they themselves believe those falsities are true. They base their reasoning and defense on mistaken impressions from the senses that the public finds captivating and convincing.

Sense-oriented people are more deceptive and ill intentioned than others.

Misers, adulterers, and deceitful people are especially sense-oriented, although before the world they appear smart.

The inner areas of their mind are disgusting and filthy; they use them to communicate with the hells. In the Word they are called the dead.

The inhabitants of hell are sense-oriented. The more sense-oriented they are, the deeper in hell they are. The sphere of hellish spirits is connected to the sensory level of our mind through a kind of back door. In the light of heaven the backs of their heads look hollowed out.

The ancients had a term for people who debate on the basis of sense impressions alone: they called them serpents of the tree of the knowledge [of good and evil].

Sense impressions ought to have the lowest priority, not the highest. For wise and intelligent people, sense impressions do have the lowest priority and are subservient to things that are deep inside. For unwise people, sense impressions have the highest priority and are in control.

If sense impressions have the lowest priority, they help open a pathway for the understanding. We then extrapolate truths by a method of extraction.

Sense impressions stand closest to the world and admit information that is coming in from it; they sift through that information.

We are in touch with the world by means of sense impressions and with heaven by means of impressions on our rationality.

Sense impressions supply things that serve the inner realms of the mind.

There are sense impressions that feed the understanding and sense impressions that feed the will.

Unless our thought is lifted above the level of our sense impressions, we have very little wisdom. When our thinking rises above sense impressions, it enters a clearer light and eventually comes into the light of heaven. From this light we become aware of things that are flowing down into us from heaven.

The outermost contents of our understanding are earthly information. The outermost contents of our will are sensory pleasures.

Our earthly self is like an animal. Over the course of our lives we take on the image of an animal. Because of this, sense-oriented people in the spiritual world appear surrounded by animals of every kind. These animals are correspondences.

Regarded on its own, our earthly self is only an animal, but because a spiritual level has been added to it we are capable of becoming human. If we decline to undergo this transformation, even though we have the faculties that make it possible, we can still pretend to be human although we are then actually just animals that can talk. In that case our talking is based on earthly rationality, but our thinking is based on spiritual insanity; our actions are based on earthly morality, but our love is based on spiritual satyriasis. To someone else who has a rationality that is spiritual, our actions seem almost exactly like the frenzied dancing of someone bitten by a tarantula, called Saint Vitus's or Saint Guy's dance.

As we all know, a hypocrite can talk about God, a robber can talk about honesty, an adulterer can talk about being a faithful spouse, and so on. We have the ability to close and open the door that stands between what we think and what we say, and the door that stands between what we intend and what we do (the doorkeeper is prudence or else deceitfulness). Without the ability to close these doors, we would quickly fall into acts of wickedness and cruelty with greater savagery than any animal. That door is opened in us all after death, though, and then it becomes apparent what we truly are. Then the forces that keep us in check are punishment and imprisonment in hell.

Therefore, kind reader, take a look inside yourself, diligently search out one evil or another within yourself, and turn away from it for religious reasons. If you turn away from it for any other reason or purpose, you are doing so only so that it will no longer appear before the world.

REFORMATION AND REGENERATION

Now that repentance has been treated, the next topic in order is our reformation and regeneration. These two both follow our repentance and are moved forward by it.

There are two states that we all inevitably enter into and go through if we are to turn from an earthly person into a spiritual person. The first state is called *reformation;* the second is called *regeneration.* In the first state we look from our earthly self toward having a spiritual self; being spiritual is what we long for. In the second state we become someone who is both spiritual and earthly. The first state is brought about by truths (these have to be truths related to faith); through these truths we aim to develop goodwill. The second state is brought about by good actions that come from goodwill; through these actions we come [more deeply] into truths related to faith.

To put it another way, the first state is a state of thought that occurs in our understanding; the second state is a state of love that occurs in our will. As the second state begins and progresses, a change takes place in our minds. There is a reversal, because then the love in our will flows into our understanding and leads and drives it to think in agreement and harmony with what we love. As good actions that come from love take on a primary role, and the truths related to faith are relegated to a secondary role, we become spiritual and are a new creation [2 Corinthians 5:17; Galatians 6:15]. Then our actions come from goodwill and our words come from faith; we develop a sense of the goodness that comes from goodwill and a perception of the truth that is related to faith; and we are in the Lord and in a state of peace. In brief, we are reborn.

If we begin the first state while we are in this world, we can be brought into the second state after we die. If we do not begin the first state while we are in this world, we cannot be brought into the second state or be reborn after we die.

These two states can be compared to the increase of light and heat that occurs as the day progresses in springtime. The first state is like the early light before dawn, when the rooster crows. The second state is like the dawn and the morning. The further development within the second state is like the increase of light and heat as the day progresses toward noon.

These two states can also be compared to the growth of grain crops. In the first stage they are like grass; after that they develop ears or fruiting spikes; and finally the grain itself grows within those structures.

These two states can also be compared to the growth of a tree. It begins as a sprout growing out of a seed in the ground. This then becomes a shoot. Then branches form and are adorned with leaves. Then the tree blossoms and fruit begins to grow in the heart of the flowers. As the fruit grows and develops, it produces new seeds, which are in effect the tree's offspring.

The first state, the state of reformation, can be compared to the state of a silkworm when it draws silky threads out of itself and wraps itself in them. After all its hard work [of transformation], it becomes able to fly in the air and feeds no longer on leaves as before but on the nectar of flowers. . . .

THE LORD ALONE CREATES US ANEW

The sections on goodwill and faith have already shown that the Lord carries out the process of regenerating us by means of goodwill and faith. . . . Both of these things, goodwill and faith, I call *means* because they forge our partnership with the

Lord. Together they ensure that our goodwill is real goodwill and that our faith is real faith. The process of our regeneration cannot occur without our having some part to play in it.

In preceding chapters, our cooperation with the Lord has come up several times; it will be illustrated again here, however, because the human mind is by nature unable to rid itself of the sensation that it carries out this process under its own power.

In every motion and every action there is an element that is active and another element that is responsive. The active element acts, and then the responsive element acts in response. As a result, a single action comes forth from the two elements. A mill is activated in this manner by a waterwheel; a carriage by a horse; a motion by a force; an effect by a cause; a dead force by a living force; and in general an instrumental cause by a principal cause. Everyone knows that each pair together completes a single action.

In the case of goodwill and faith, the Lord acts, and we act in response. There is an activity of the Lord that prompts our human response. The power to do good things comes from the Lord. As a result, there is a will to act that seems to be our own, because we have free choice. Either we can take action together with the Lord and by doing so, form a partnership with him; or else we can take action drawing on the power of hell, which is outside the Lord, and by doing so, separate ourselves from him. Actions of ours that are in harmony with the Lord's actions are what I mean here by "cooperation." To make this even clearer, it will be illustrated with comparisons below.

It follows from this that the Lord is constantly active in regenerating us. He is constantly active in saving us, and no one can be saved without being regenerated, as the Lord himself says in John: "Those who are not born again cannot see the kingdom of God" (John 3:3, 5, 6). Regeneration is therefore the means of being saved; and goodwill and faith are the means of being regenerated.

The notion that we are regenerated as a consequence of simply having the faith that is preached by the church of today—a faith that involves no cooperation on our part—is the height of foolishness.

The kind of action and cooperation just described is visible in action and movement of all types. The interaction between the heart and all its arteries is an example. The heart acts and the arteries use their sheaths and linings to cooperate; this results in circulation. A similar thing happens with the lungs. The air pressure, which depends on the height of the atmosphere above it, acts upon the lungs; the lungs work the ribs, which is immediately followed by the ribs working the lungs. This breathing motion affects every membrane in the body. The meninges of the brain, the pleura, the peritoneum, the diaphragm, and all the other membranes that cover the internal organs and inwardly hold them together, act and react and cooperate in this way, because they are flexible. Together these movements provide for our continued existence.

A similar thing happens in every fiber and nerve and in every muscle. In fact it even occurs in every piece of cartilage. It is well documented that in each of these there is an [initiating] action and then a cooperation.

Such cooperation also exists in all our bodily senses. Just like the motor organs, the sensory organs consist of fibers, membranes, and muscles; but there is no need to describe the cooperation of each one. It is well known that light acts upon the eye, sound upon the ear, odor upon the nose, taste upon the tongue; and that the organs adapt themselves to that input, which results in sensation.

Surely everyone can see from these examples that thought and will could not exist unless there was a similar action and cooperation between life as it inflows and the spiritual organic structure underlying our brain. Life flows from the Lord into that organic structure. Because the organic structure cooperates, it perceives what it is thinking. Likewise it perceives what is under consideration there, what conclusion is formed, and what action it has decided to take. If the life force alone took action but we did not cooperate (seemingly on our own), our ability to think would not exceed a log's. We would have no more thought than a church building does when a minister is preaching; the church can indeed feel the reverberation of sound coming through the double doors as an echo, but it cannot appreciate anything about the sermon. We would be no different if we did not cooperate with the Lord in developing goodwill and faith.

What we would be like if we did not cooperate with the Lord can be further illustrated with the following comparisons. If we perceived or sensed anything spiritual related to heaven or the church, it would strike us as something hostile or disagreeable flowing in, the way our nose would react to a rotten smell, our ear would react to a dissonant sound, our eye would react to a hideous sight, or our tongue would react to something disgusting.

If the delight associated with goodwill and the enjoyment associated with faith were to flow into the spiritual organic structure of the mind of people who take delight in evil and falsity, such people would feel terrible pain and torment until they eventually collapsed in unconsciousness. The spiritual organic structure consists of long strands in helixes; under that circumstance in people of that type, it would wrap itself in coils and would be tormented like a snake on a swarm of ants. The truth of this has been fully demonstrated to me in the spiritual world through an abundance of experiences. . . .

REGENERATION PROGRESSES IN THE SAME WAY THAT OUR BODY DEVELOPS

For human beings, there is a constant correspondence between the stages a person goes through physically and the stages a person goes through spiritually, or developments in the body and developments in the spirit. The reason is that at the level of our souls we are born spiritual, but we are clothed with earthly material that constitutes our physical body. When our physical body is laid aside, our soul, which has its own spiritual body, enters a world in which all things are spiritual. There we associate with other spiritual beings like ourselves.

Our spiritual body has to be formed within our physical body. The spiritual body is made out of truth and goodness that flow into us from the Lord through the spiritual world. We find a home within ourselves for that goodness and truth in things that parallel them in the physical world, which are called civic and moral forms of goodness and truth. This makes clear, then, the nature of the process that forms our spiritual body.

Since there is a constant correspondence within human beings between the stages we go through physically and the stages we go through spiritually, it follows that we go through something analogous to being conceived, carried in the womb, born, and brought up.

This explains why the statements in the Word that relate to physical birth symbolize aspects of our spiritual birth that have to do with goodness and truth. In fact, every earthly reference in the literal sense of the Word embodies, contains, and symbolizes something spiritual.

The earthly references to birth in the Word inwardly refer to our spiritual birth, as anyone can see from the following passages:

> We have conceived; we have gone into labor. We appeared to give birth, yet we have not accomplished salvation. (Isaiah 26:18)

> You are having birth pangs, O earth, in the presence of the Lord. (Psalms 114:7)

> Will the earth give birth in a single day? Will I break [waters] but not cause delivery? Will I cause delivery and then close [the womb]? (Isaiah 66:7–9)

Pains like those of a woman in labor will come upon Ephraim. He is an unwise son, because he does not remain long in the womb for children. (Hosea 13:12, 13)

Many similar passages occur elsewhere.

Since physical birth in the Word symbolizes spiritual birth, and spiritual birth comes from the Lord, he is called our Maker and the one who delivered us from the womb, as is clear from the following passages.

Jehovah, who made you and formed you in the womb . . . (Isaiah 44:2)

You delivered me from the womb. (Psalms 22:9)

On you I was laid from the womb. You delivered me from my mother's belly. (Psalms 71:6)

Listen to me, you whom I carried from the womb, whom I bore from the womb. (Isaiah 46:3)

There are other such passages as well.

This is why the Lord is called the Father, as in Isaiah 9:6; 63:16; John 10:30; 14:8, 9. This is why people who have received things that are good and true from the Lord are called "children of God" and "those who are born of God," and why they are said to be siblings to each other (Matthew 23:8). This is also why the church is referred to as a mother (Hosea 2:2, 5; Ezekiel 16:45).

The above points make it clear that there is a correspondence between physical birth and spiritual birth. Because there is this correspondence, it follows that not only can we speak of this new birth as including stages of being conceived, being carried in the womb, being born, and being brought up, but those stages of our rebirth are actually real. What exactly the stages are, however, will be presented in proper sequence as this chapter on regeneration unfolds.

Here I will just mention that human seed is conceived inwardly within the understanding and takes shape within the will. From there it is transferred into the testicles, where it wraps itself in an earthly covering. Then it is delivered to the womb and finally enters the world.

There is also a correspondence between human regeneration and every aspect of the plant kingdom. This is why the Word portrays us as *trees,* the truth we have as *seed,* and the goodness we have as *fruit.*

A bad species of tree can be born anew, so to speak, and afterward bear good fruit and good seed; this is clear from grafting. Even though the bad sap rises from the root through the stem all the way to the point where the graft was made, it nevertheless turns into good sap and makes the tree good. A similar thing happens with people who are grafted onto the Lord, as he teaches with the following words:

> I am the vine; you are the branches. Those who live in me and I in them bear much fruit. If any do not live in me, they are cast out as branches. Once dried they are thrown into the fire. (John 15:5, 6)

Many scholars have pointed out the parallels between human reproduction and the reproduction not just of trees but of all plants. I will add something on the subject here to wrap up this discussion.

Among trees and all other members of the plant kingdom there are not two sexes—masculine and feminine. There is just one sex, which is masculine. The ground or earth alone is a mother to them all, and is therefore like a woman. The ground receives the seeds of plants of all kinds. It opens those seeds, carries them as in a womb, nourishes them, and gives birth to them—that is, brings them forth into daylight. Afterward it clothes them and sustains them.

Once the seed has opened in the earth, it first develops a root, which is like a heart. From the root it sends out sap, which is like blood. By so doing it makes a kind of body complete with limbs: the body is the trunk; its limbs are the branches and twigs. The leaves that the plant unfurls immediately after its birth play the role of the lungs. Just as the heart cannot produce motion or sensation without the help of the lungs, but with their help brings us to life, the root cannot develop into a tree or a plant without the help of the leaves. The flowers, which are the first steps toward fruit, are a means of refining the sap (the "blood" of the plant) by separating the purer elements from elements that are impure, and then forming a new stem to allow the purer elements to flow into the center of the flowers. The purified sap then flows through this stem and begins to construct and then mature the fruit. The fruit is like a testicle; the seeds mature within it.

The plant soul (or to put it another way, the plant's prolific essence), which is dominant at the inmost level within every drop of sap, comes from no other source than the heat of the spiritual world. Because this heat originates in the spiritual sun, its constant goal is to generate [new life] and therefore ensure that creation continues. Because this heat has the generation of new people as its essential aim, therefore whatever it generates bears some resemblance to humankind.

In case you are surprised by my saying that all the inhabitants of the plant kingdom are masculine and that only the earth or the ground plays the role of woman or mother to all, I will use the illustration of a similar situation among bees. According to Swammerdam's eyewitness account, as presented in his *Book of Nature,* there is only one common mother who produces all the offspring within a whole hive. If these little creatures have but one common mother, why should that not be the case with all plants?

The idea that the earth is a mother to all can also be illustrated spiritually. The "earth" in the Word means the church, and the church is a mother to all, and is even called that in the Word [Galatians 4:26]. For evidence that *earth* means the church, see the discussion of this word in *Revelation Unveiled* §§285, 902.

The reason why the earth or ground is able to infiltrate the center of a seed, including its prolific material, and bring this out and circulate it, is that every little grain of dirt or pollen exudes from its essence a subtle emanation, which penetrates the seed. This infiltration is a result of the active force of the heat from the spiritual world.

We can be regenerated only gradually. Each and every thing that exists in the physical world serves as an illustration of this fact. A seedling does not grow up into a mature tree in a single day. First there is a seed, then a root, then a shoot, which develops into a trunk; then branches come out of that and develop leaves and finally flowers and fruit. Wheat and barley do not spring up ready for harvest in a single day. A home is not built in a single day. We do not become full grown in a single day; reaching wisdom takes us even longer. The church is not established—let alone perfected—in a single day. We will make no progress toward a goal unless we first make a start.

People who have a different conception than this of regeneration know nothing about goodwill or faith, or how each of these qualities grows as we cooperate with the Lord. All this makes clear that regeneration progresses analogously to the way we are conceived, carried in the womb, born, and brought up.

REFORMATION HAPPENS IN OUR UNDERSTANDING, REGENERATION IN OUR WILL

Because this heading and headings to follow concern reformation and regeneration, and reformation pertains to the understanding but regeneration pertains to the will, it is important for you to know the difference between the understanding and the will. The difference between them has been laid out [at the beginning of the first chapter of this book]. Therefore I recommend that you read that section first, and then read what is here.

The evils we are born with are in the will that is part of our earthly self; this earthly will pressures the understanding to agree with it and to have thoughts that harmonize with its desires. Therefore if we are to be regenerated, this has to happen by means of our understanding as an intermediate cause.

This process draws on pieces of information that our understanding receives, first from our parents and teachers, and later from our reading the Word, listening to preaching, reading books, and having conversations. The things that our understanding receives as a result are called truths. Therefore to say that we are reformed by means of our understanding is the same as saying that we are reformed by means of truths that our understanding receives. Truths teach us who to believe in, what to believe, and also what to do and what to will. After all, whatever we do, we do from our will and in accordance with our understanding.

Since our will is evil from the day we are born, and since our understanding teaches us what is evil and what is good and that it is possible for us to will one and not the other, it follows that our understanding is the means by which we have to be reformed. During the phase called our reformation, we come to mentally see and admit that evil is evil and goodness is good, and make the decision to choose what is good. When we actually try to abstain from evil and do what is good, the phase called our regeneration begins.

For this purpose we have been granted the ability to lift our understanding almost all the way into the light enjoyed by the angels in heaven. This lifting allows us to see what we ought to will and what we ought to do in order to be successful during our time in this world and blessed with happiness after death to eternity. We become successful and blessed if we gain wisdom for ourselves and keep our will obedient to that wisdom. We become unsuccessful and unhappy, however, if we devote our understanding to obeying our will. The reason for this is that from the time we are born, our will has a tendency toward evils of various kinds, including evils that are horrendous. If our will was not restrained by our understanding and instead we let it run free, we would quickly fall into criminal behavior; because of our inborn savage animal nature, for purely selfish reasons we would wipe out and butcher everyone and anyone who failed to show us favor or indulge our lusts.

For another thing, if our understanding were incapable of being perfected on its own and of then perfecting our will, we would not be human at all; we would be animals. If there were no separation between our will and our understanding and if the understanding could not rise above the will, we would be unable either to think or to say what we thought. We would only be able to make noises that expressed our feelings. We would not be able to act in reasonable ways, either; we would act on instinct alone. We would be completely incapable of knowing anything about God or seeing him through what we knew; as a result, we would be unable to form a partnership with him and live forever.

We have thoughts and we will things as if we did so on our own. This feeling that we think and will on our own is what allows for a reciprocal partnership [with the Lord]. No partnership can exist without reciprocation. For example, no partnership would exist between an active element and a responsive element if there were no adaptation or point of contact between them.

God alone is an active force. We allow ourselves to experience that active force and we cooperate with it to all appearances as if we were acting on our own, although inwardly we are actually acting from God.

From the statements just made, if you take them in the right way, you can see what human beings are like. You can see the quality of love the human will has if it is lifted up by means of the understanding; and you can see the quality of love the human will has if it is not lifted up.

It is important to know that the capacity to lift the understanding even to the level possessed by the angels in heaven has been created as a part of every human being, the evil as well as the good. In fact every devil in hell retains this ability, since all those who are in hell existed as human beings [in the physical world]. I have often been shown through living experience that this is the case.

Nonetheless, the reason the devils in hell are insane rather than intelligent in spiritual matters is that they will what is evil and not what is good. Knowing and understanding truths is repulsive to them, because truths favor what is good and oppose what is evil.

These points also make it clear that the first step in our being generated anew is to receive truths in our understanding. The second step is to intend to put those truths into practice; eventually it takes the form of actually putting them into practice.

No one can justifiably be called a "reformed" person solely on the basis of his or her knowledge of truth. By lifting our understanding above the love that resides in our will, we are all capable of grasping those truths, saying them, teaching them, and preaching them. A truly reformed person is someone who desires the truth because it is true. This desire attaches itself to our will, and if it persists, forges a partnership between our will and our understanding. Then our regeneration begins. (Later sections will deal with how our regeneration proceeds and is perfected after that.)

The following comparisons can illustrate what people are like when their understanding has been lifted up but the love in their will has not. They are like an eagle that soars on high, but as soon as it sees something to eat below, such as hens, cygnets, or even little lambs, it drops like a stone and devours them.

They are also like an adulterous husband who has a whore hidden in his basement. He keeps going back and forth to the top level of his house. Up there in the presence of his wife he says wise things to his guests about faithfulness in marriage, but now and then suddenly leaves to go downstairs and satisfy his lewd desires with his whore.

They are also like swamp flies that fly in a column above the head of a running horse. Once the horse stops, they plunge back into their swamp.

This is what we are like when our understanding is lifted up but the love in our will remains below, near our feet, immersed in the unclean desires of its nature and lusting for sensual gratification.

Because people in this state shine intellectually as if they possessed wisdom and yet their will is contrary to wisdom, they are like snakes with scales that reflect the light, or like beetles that shine as if they were made of gold. They are also like the strange light over swamps at night, or from the glow of rotting wood, or from phosphorus.

Some who are in this state can masquerade as angels of light, both among people in this world and, after they die, among angels of heaven. After a brief examination there, however, their clothes are removed and they are thrown out naked. They cannot be detected in this world, because here their spirit is not visible; it is covered over with a mask, like the one a comic actor wears on stage. The fact that they can use their faces and words to masquerade as angels of light is both a result and a sign of the fact that they can lift their understanding almost all the way into angelic wisdom, above the love in their will, as I mentioned before. Since our inner and our outer self can go in opposite directions like this, and because our body is cast off but our spirit remains, it is clear then that a dark spirit can live behind a bright face, and a raging spirit can lie behind soothing words.

Therefore, my friend, know people for what they are, not by their mouth but by their heart—that is, not from what they say but from what they do. The Lord says, "Beware of false prophets who come to you in sheep's clothing but are inwardly as predatory as wolves. Recognize them by their fruits" (Matthew 7:15, 16).

OUR INNER SELF HAS TO BE REFORMED FIRST, THEN OUR OUTER SELF

. . . The concepts of the inner and outer self taught by the new church are completely different [from what is taught by other churches]. In this view, our inner self is our will. It is the source of the thoughts we have when we are left to ourselves, such as when we are at home. Our outer self is what we do and say in company or in public. Our inner self, then, is goodwill and faith—goodwill that belongs to our will, and faith that occupies our thoughts.

Before we undergo regeneration, goodwill and faith constitute our earthly self, which is divided into an inner and an outer level. This is clear from the fact that we are not allowed to act in company or in public the way we do when left to ourselves at home. What causes the split into an inner and outer level is that civil law prescribes punishments for those who do evil things and rewards for those who do good things. Since no one wants to be punished and everyone wants to be rewarded, we therefore force ourselves to create an outer self that is separate from our inner self. The reward takes the form of wealth or a good reputation; we achieve neither one unless we live according to the law. This is why morality and benevolence are practiced outwardly, even by people who have no morality or benevolence inwardly. This is the origin of all hypocrisy, flattery, and pretense.

As for the earthly self being split into two levels, this is an actual division of both will and thought. Every action that we take originates in our will; every word we say originates in our thought. Below our first earthly will, we ourselves create a second will and a second thought process, which also belong to our earthly self. The will that we create ourselves could be called our *bodily* will, because it drives the body to behave in moral ways. The thought process that we create ourselves could be called *lung-related* thought, because it drives our lips and tongue to say things that show a good understanding.

Taken together, this type of thought and this will can be compared to the inner bark that adheres to the outer bark of a tree; or it can be compared to the membrane that adheres to the shell of an egg. Behind this self-made thought and will lies the inner earthly self. If we are evil, our inner earthly self is like rotten heartwood within a tree whose outer and inner bark appears whole; or like a rotten egg inside a clean white shell.

Now to the nature of the inner earthly self that we are born with. Its will has a tendency toward evils of every kind and therefore its thinking has a tendency toward falsities of every kind. This inner self, then, is what needs to be regenerated. If it is not regenerated, it harbors hatred toward everything related to goodwill and anger at everything related to faith.

It follows, then, that our inner earthly self must be regenerated first, and our outer self must then be regenerated through our inner self. This sequence follows the divine design. To regenerate our inner self through our outer self would go contrary to the divine design, because the inner self acts as the soul of the outer self, not only in a general way but in every detail. The inner self is present in everything we say, without our even realizing it. This is what allows angels to perceive the quality of our will from a single action of ours, and the quality of our thinking from a single thing we say—the "quality" meaning whether we are hellish or heavenly. As a result, they have complete knowledge of us. From our tone of voice they perceive the interests that drive our thinking; from a gesture of ours, or the form of one action, they perceive the love that resides in our will. They detect this no matter how good we are at presenting ourselves as a Christian and a moral citizen.

Our regeneration is portrayed in Ezekiel as the dry bones on which sinews were placed; then flesh, and skin, and spirit was breathed into them, and they came to life (Ezekiel 37:1–14). The following words in that story make it obvious that it represents regeneration: "These bones are the whole house of Israel" (Ezekiel 37:11). There is also a comparison there involving graves. We read that God will open graves and cause bones to rise up out of them, and he will put spirit in them and place them in the land of Israel (Ezekiel 37:12, 13, 14). The land of Israel here and elsewhere means the church. Bones and graves were used to represent regeneration because people who have not been regenerated are called the dead, and people who have been regenerated are called the living. The former are spiritually dead, but the latter are spiritually alive.

Every created thing in the world, both animate and inanimate, has an inner level and an outer level. The one level does not exist in the absence of the other, any more than an effect can exist without a cause. Every created thing is considered valuable if it is inwardly good, and worthless if it is inwardly bad, even where inner badness lies within outer goodness. Every wise person in the world and every angel in heaven evaluates people and things in this way.

What a person who has not been regenerated is like and what a person who has been regenerated is like can be illustrated through comparisons. People who have not been regenerated but who present themselves as moral citizens and "good Christians" can be compared to a corpse that has been embalmed with fragrant oils but nevertheless gives off a reek that overpowers the fragrances, assaults your nose, and hurts your brain. . . .

In our world, of course, the inside is sometimes valued highly on the basis of what is outside, but only by people who themselves have no inner goodness and who therefore judge things by appearances. This is not how it works in heaven, however. The body that can be turned this way and that around the spirit and can be bent from evil to good is removed by death, and then only the inner self remains, which constitutes the spirit. Then even from far away such people look like a snake that has shed its skin, or rotten wood whose shiny bark has been removed. It is different, though, for those who have been regenerated. Their inner level is good and their outer level, which appears to be like anyone else's, is actually as different from that of the people just mentioned as heaven is from hell, since it has a soul of goodness inside.

After death it means nothing anymore whether people in this world were of high rank and lived in a mansion and walked around with an entourage, or lived in a hut and were waited on by a child. It does not matter if they were an archbishop who wore a scarlet robe and a two-tiered tiara, or a shepherd tending a few sheep in the woods, who wore a loose-fitting country coat with a hood for his head.

Gold is still gold whether it shines next to the fire or its surface is blackened with smoke. Gold is still gold whether it has been poured into a beautiful shape like that of a little child or an unpleasant shape like that of a rat. The rats made of gold and placed next to the ark were still found acceptable and pleasing (1 Samuel 6:3, 4, 5, and following), because gold symbolizes inner goodness. Diamonds and rubies that have been kept in their matrix of limestone or clay are just as valuable as diamonds and rubies set in a queen's necklace, because they are valued for their inner goodness. And so on.

This makes it clear that what is on the outside derives its value from what is on the inside and not the other way around.

REFORMATION LEADS TO AN INTERNAL BATTLE

The reason why a battle develops at this point [in the process of regeneration] is that our inner self has been reformed through truths. These truths allow us to see what evil and falsity are; but we still have evil and falsity in our outer or earthly self. At first, therefore, a disagreement arises between our new will, which is above, and our old will, which is below. Because these two wills are in disagreement, what they delight in is incompatible as well.

As we know, the flesh is against the spirit and the spirit against the flesh; the flesh and its lusts have to be brought under control before the spirit can become active and we can be a new person [Romans 7:22–23; Galatians 5:16–17, 24–25; Ephesians 4:22–24; 1 Peter 2:11].

After this disagreement of wills occurs, a battle develops, which is what is known as a crisis of the spirit. This inner conflict, this battle, is not between good and evil [directly], but between truths that defend what is good and falsities that defend what is evil. Goodness cannot do its own fighting; it fights through truths. Evil, too, cannot do its own fighting; it fights through falsities. Likewise, the will is unable to do its own fighting; it fights through its understanding, where its truths are kept.

That battle is something we feel inside ourselves and nowhere else; we experience it as an attack of conscience. In reality, though, it is the Lord and the Devil (meaning hell) that are fighting inside us. They fight for control over us, or to see whose we will be. The Devil, or hell, attacks us and summons the evils that are inside us. The Lord protects us and summons the good things that are inside us.

Although this battle takes place in the spiritual world, it is also a battle inside ourselves between the truths that defend what is good and the falsities that defend what is evil within us. Therefore we have to join the fight as if we were acting completely on our own. We have free choice to act either on the Lord's behalf or on the Devil's behalf. We are on the Lord's side if we stay with the truths that defend what is good. We are on the Devil's side if we stay with the falsities that defend what is evil.

It follows from this that whichever self wins, whether it is our inner self or our outer self, it will control the other. It is entirely the same as two enemy monarchs who fight over which of them is going to rule the other's country; the one who wins gains control of the other's territory, and all who live there have to obey their new ruler.

In this case, if our inner self wins it rules and gains control of all the evils in our outer self; our regeneration then continues. If on the other hand our outer self wins, it rules and drives away all the good qualities in our inner self; our regeneration then ceases.

There is some recognition today that crises of the spirit exist, but hardly anyone knows what causes them, what they are like, or what good they do. What causes them and what they are like was just covered above; so was the good they do. That is, when our inner self wins, it gains control of our outer self. Once this is under control, our lusts are uprooted. Desires for goodness and truth are planted in their place, arranged in such a way that the good and true things we will and think about we also practice and speak about from the heart. In addition, through victory over our outer self we become spiritual and the Lord brings us into association with the angels of heaven, all of whom are spiritual. . . .

The feeling of contrition that is claimed to precede the faith of today is not a crisis of the spirit. I have asked many about it, and they said that it is a word and nothing more, unless it is perhaps some fearful thought on the part of ordinary people when they contemplate the fires of hell.

Once the conflict is over, we are present in heaven in our inner self and present in the world through our outer self. Therefore crises of the spirit accomplish a joining of heaven and the world within us. Then the Lord within us rules our world from our heaven, following the divine design.

The opposite happens if we remain earthly. Then we greatly desire to rule heaven from our world. All who have a love for power that comes from loving themselves are like this. If we are examined inwardly, it is discovered that we do not believe in any god, but only in ourselves. After death, we believe that we *are* a god who has greater power than others. This is the kind of insanity that exists in hell. It falls to such a depth that some there say they are God the Father, some say they are God the Son, and others say they are God the Holy Spirit. Some Jews there say they are the Messiah. This makes it clear what we are like after death if our earthly self is not regenerated. It shows what we would imagine ourselves to be if a new church were not established, in which things that are genuinely true are taught. This is the topic of the following words of the Lord: "At the close of the age," meaning the end of the church of today, "there will be a great affliction such as has never existed since the world began until now and will never exist again. In fact, unless those days were cut short no flesh would be saved" (Matthew 24:3, 21, 22).

While he was in the world, the Lord glorified his human manifestation, that is, made it divine, through battles and inner conflict. In a similar way within us individually, the Lord fights for us while we are undergoing inner conflict and conquers the hellish spirits who are assaulting us. Afterward he "glorifies" us, that is, makes us spiritual.

After his universal redemption, the Lord restructured all things in heaven and in hell in accordance with the divine design. He does much the same thing in us after crises of the spirit—that is, he restructures all the things in us that relate to heaven and the world in accordance with the divine design.

After his redemption, the Lord established a new church. Likewise, he establishes the principles of the church in us and turns us into an individual church.

After redemption, the Lord granted peace to those who believed in him. He said, "I leave my peace with you; I give my peace to you. I do not give to you the way the world gives" (John 14:27). In much the same way, after we have undergone a crisis of the spirit he allows us to feel peace, that is, gladness of mind and consolation.

From all this it is clear that the Lord is the Redeemer to eternity.

If our inner self alone were regenerated and not our outer self at the same time, we could be compared to a bird flying in the air that can find no place to rest on dry ground but only in a swamp, where it is attacked by snakes and frogs, and it flies away and dies. . . .

We could also be compared to a house without a foundation, or a column without a footing to support it.

This is what we would be like if our inner self alone were reformed but not our outer self at the same time. We would have no outlet through which to do what is good.

WHEN WE HAVE BEEN REGENERATED, WE HAVE A NEW WILL AND A NEW UNDERSTANDING

When we have been regenerated we are renewed, or new. This is something the church of today knows, both from *the Word* and from *reason*.

We know this from the following teachings in *the Word*.

Make your heart new and your spirit new. Why should you die, O house of Israel? (Ezekiel 18:31)

I will give you a new heart and I will put a new spirit within you. I will remove the heart of stone from your flesh and give you a heart of flesh. I will put my spirit within you. (Ezekiel 36:26, 27)

From now on we regard no one on the basis of the flesh. Therefore if anyone is in Christ, she or he is a new creation. (2 Corinthians 5:16, 17)

The *new heart* in these passages means a new will and the *new spirit* means a new understanding, since "heart" in the Word means the will and "spirit," when it appears alongside "heart," means the understanding.

From *reason* as well we know about our renewal: the person who has been regenerated must have a new will and a new understanding, because these two faculties are what make us human. They are the parts of us that are regenerated. The quality of these two faculties determines the quality of the human being. People who have an evil will are evil; if their understanding supports that will, they are even more evil. The opposite is true of good people.

Only religion renews and regenerates us. It is allotted the highest place in the human mind. Below itself it sees civic concerns that relate to the world. In fact, it rises up through these concerns the way the purest sap rises up through a tree to its very top, and surveys from that height the earthly things that lie below, the way someone looks down from a tower or a high point of land onto the fields below.

It is important to note, however, that our understanding can rise up almost into the light that the angels of heaven have, but if our will does not rise along with it, we are still the old self, not the new self. (I have already shown how the understanding lifts the will up with itself, higher and higher.) For this reason, regeneration is primarily a matter of the will, and only secondarily a matter of the understanding. The understanding in us is like light in the world, and our will is like the heat here. Without heat, light brings nothing to life and makes nothing grow; as we know, light has to act in partnership with heat. The understanding that is in the lower part of the mind is actually in the light of this world; the understanding that is in the higher part of the mind is in the light of heaven. Therefore if our will is not lifted up from the lower region into the higher region to join the understanding, it remains at the level of the world. Then our understanding flies up and down, up and down. Every night, though, it flies down and sleeps with our will below, and the two make love like a married man and a whore and bring forth two-headed offspring.

Again, it is clear that if we do not have a new will and a new understanding, we have not been regenerated.

The human mind has three levels. The lowest is called the earthly level; the middle is called the spiritual level; the highest is called the heavenly level. As we are regenerated, we are lifted from the lowest level, which is earthly, onto the higher level that is spiritual, and from there onto the heavenly level. (The existence of three levels within the mind will be demonstrated under the next heading).

As a result, someone who has not been regenerated is called earthly, but someone who has been regenerated is called spiritual. Clearly, then, the mind of someone who has been regenerated is lifted up to the spiritual level. From up there it sees what is going on in the earthly mind below.

By paying even slight attention to our own thoughts, any of us can see and admit that there is a lower level and a higher level within the human mind. After all, we can see what we are thinking. Therefore we say, "I was thinking this or that, and now I am thinking something else." We could never do this if there were not an inner level of thought, called perception, which can carefully examine our lower level of thought, called thinking.

When judges hear or read arguments that a lawyer has laid out in a long chain, they bring them together into one view, one all-encompassing image, in the higher level of their mind. Then they direct their attention toward the lower level, where earthly thought occurs, and they arrange the arguments into a sequence and hand down a sentence or judgment based on their higher vision.

Surely everyone realizes that we are capable of having thoughts or making decisions in a moment or two that take half an hour to put into words through our lower thought.

I present these examples to make it known that the human mind has higher and lower levels.

As for the new will, it is above the old will, on the spiritual level. So is the new understanding. The understanding is with the will and the will is with the understanding. They come together on that level, and together they examine the old, earthly self and arrange all the things in it so that they obey what is higher.

Surely everyone can see what would happen if there were only one level to the human mind—evil traits and good traits would be brought together and mixed up with each other there, as well as false impressions and true impressions, and conflict would erupt. It would be like putting wolves and sheep, or tigers and calves, or hawks and doves together in the same cage. The inevitable outcome would be a cruel slaughter, in which the savage animals tore the gentle ones to pieces.

Therefore it has been provided that good things along with their truths are gathered on a higher level so that they can remain safe and ward off an attack, and can use chains and other means to bring evils under control and finally disperse them along with their falsities.

This is the point made in an earlier section, that the Lord through heaven rules the things of this world that are present in a regenerated person. The higher or spiritual level of the human mind is in fact a heaven in miniature form, and the lower or earthly level is the world in miniature form. This is why the ancients referred to the human being as a microcosm. We could also be called a microheaven.

People who have been regenerated, that is, people who have been made anew in will and understanding, are in the heat of heaven; that is, they have the love that heaven has. They are also in the light of heaven; that is, they have the wisdom heaven has. On the other hand, people who have not been regenerated are in the heat of hell; that is, they have the love that hell has. They are also in the darkness of hell; that is, they have the insanities that hell has.

Nowadays this is well known, yet in other ways it is not known, because the church as it exists today has made regeneration an appendage to its faith. It says that reasoning should not be applied to the subject of faith, and should therefore not be applied to anything that is an appendage to faith, namely, regeneration and renewal.

To people [in the church today], regeneration and renewal, along with that faith itself, are like a house whose doors and windows have been boarded up. No one knows who or what is inside the house. It may be empty; it might be full of demons from hell, or angels from heaven.

In addition, confusion has been caused by a misinterpretation of the fact that we can rise up with our understanding almost into the light of heaven and therefore think and speak intelligently about spiritual matters, no matter what the love in our will is like. Not knowing the truth of this situation has led to complete ignorance about what it is to be regenerated and made new.

From the above we can conclude that when we have not been regenerated, we see ghosts at night, so to speak, and think they are real people. When we are being regenerated, we become aware first thing in the morning that what was seen in the night was unreal. When we have been regenerated and are in broad daylight, we realize that our visions in the night were a form of madness.

People who have not been regenerated are dreaming; people who have been regenerated are awake. In fact, in the Word our earthly life is compared to a sleep and our spiritual life to wakefulness. . . .

REGENERATED PEOPLE ARE IN FELLOWSHIP WITH THE ANGELS OF HEAVEN

Every human being is in fellowship, that is, in close association, with either angels of heaven or spirits of hell, because we are born to become spiritual, and we cannot become spiritual unless we are associated with others who are spiritual. In the work *Heaven and Hell* I have shown that our minds are in both worlds, the physical and the spiritual.

Nevertheless both the people and the angels or spirits are unaware of this connection, because as long as we remain alive in this world, we are in an earthly state, whereas the angels and spirits are in a spiritual state. Because of the differences between what is earthly and what is spiritual, neither one of us appears to the other. The nature of the differences is described in the memorable occurrence recorded in *Marriage Love* §§326–329. That passage makes it clear that it is not our thoughts but rather our feelings that form a connection between us. Yet hardly any of us reflect on our feelings, because they are not in the light of our understanding and thought; they are instead in the warmth of our will and of the emotions that relate to what we love. Nevertheless, the connection that is established by feelings of love held in common between people on the one hand and angels and spirits on the other is so tight that if it were broken and the angels and spirits were separated from us, we would immediately lose consciousness. If that relationship were not reestablished and angels and spirits were not reconnected to us, we would die.

When I say that we become "spiritual" as a result of being regenerated, I do not mean that we [who are still in the physical world] become as fully spiritual as angels; I mean that we become both spiritual and earthly, meaning that within our earthly self there is a spiritual self, which is present in much the same way thought is present in speech or the will is present in action—if one stops, the other stops. Similarly, our spirit is present in the individual things our body does. The spirit is what drives the earthly component to do what it does. Viewed on its own, the earthly part of us is something passive; it is a dead force. The spiritual part of us is something active; it is a living force. Something passive, a dead force, cannot take action on its own. It must be driven by something active, a living force.

Since we live constantly in fellowship with inhabitants of the spiritual world, as soon as we leave the physical world we are immediately placed among the spirits like ourselves whom we had been with while in the world. This is why all of us after we die seem to ourselves to be still alive in the world—we come into contact with people who have the same feelings as we do in our will. We claim these spirits as "our people," just as friends and neighbors in this world claim each other as "their people." This is what the Word means when it says that those who die are gathered to their people.

These points establish the fact that people who have been regenerated are in fellowship with the angels of heaven, whereas people who have not been regenerated are in fellowship with the spirits of hell.

It is important to know that there are three heavens and that they are divided up according to three levels of love and wisdom. As we progress in our regeneration we come into fellowship with angels from those three heavens. Because this is the case, the human mind, too, has three levels or areas just like the heavens. (For more on the three heavens and their division according to the three levels of love and wisdom, see *Heaven and Hell* §29 and following; see also the little work *Soul-Body Interaction* §§16, 17.)

Here the nature of the three levels into which the heavens are divided will be illustrated only by a comparison. They are like the head, the upper body, and the lower body in a person. The highest heaven constitutes the head; the middle heaven, the upper body; and the lowest heaven, the lower body. In fact, the whole of heaven in the Lord's sight is like one human being. The truth of this has been disclosed to me through firsthand experience: I was given permission to see an entire community of heaven, which consisted of tens of thousands of angels, as one human being. Why would the whole of heaven not appear that way before the Lord? For more on this living experience, see *Heaven and Hell* §59 and following.

This also clarifies how we should understand the well-known saying in the Christian world that the church constitutes the body of Christ, and that Christ is the life within this body. It serves as well to illustrate the point that the Lord is everything to all heaven, since he is the life within that body. The Lord is also the life within the church that exists among people who acknowledge him alone as the God of heaven and earth and who believe in him. (He himself teaches, in Matthew 28:18, that he is the God of heaven and earth, and in John 3:15, 16, 36; 6:40; and 11:25, 26, that we are to believe in him.)

The three levels on which the heavens exist, and therefore on which the human mind exists, can to some extent be illustrated by physical things in our world. The three levels are like the relative differences in value between gold, silver, and copper. (The statue of Nebuchadnezzar, Daniel 2:31 and following, is another analogy that uses these metals.) These three levels are as different from each other as a ruby, a sapphire, and an agate are different in purity and value. An olive tree, a grapevine, and a fig tree would be another set of examples; and so on. In fact, in the Word, gold, a ruby, and an olive tree symbolize goodness that is heavenly, the type of goodness found in the highest heaven; silver, a sapphire, and a grapevine symbolize goodness that is spiritual, the type of goodness found in the middle heaven; and copper, an agate, and a fig tree symbolize goodness that is earthly, the type of goodness found in the lowest heaven. (I have shown above that the three levels are the heavenly, the spiritual, and the earthly.)

The following needs to be added to what has been stated so far: Our regeneration does not happen in a moment. It gradually unfolds from the beginning all the way to the end of our lives in this world; and after this life is over, it continues and is perfected.

Because we are reformed through battles and victories against the evils of our flesh, the Son of Humankind says to each of the seven churches that gifts will be given to those who overcome. That is, to the church in Ephesus he says, "To those who overcome I will give [food] to eat from the tree of life" (Revelation 2:7). To the church in Smyrna he says, "Those who overcome will suffer no harm from the second death" (Revelation 2:11). To the church in Pergamos he says, "To those who overcome I will give the hidden manna to eat" (Revelation 2:17). To the church in Thyatira he says, "To those who overcome I will give power over the nations" (Revelation 2:26). To the church in Sardis he says, "Those who overcome will be clothed in white garments" (Revelation 3:5). To the church in Philadelphia he says, "Those who overcome I will make pillars in the temple of God" (Revelation 3:12). To the church in Laodicea he says, "To those who overcome I will grant to sit with me on my throne" (Revelation 3:21).

Let me also add the following as a final note: The more we are reborn, that is, the more the process of regeneration is perfected in us, the less we attribute anything of goodness and truth, or goodwill and faith, to ourselves; we attribute it all to the Lord. We are taught this very clearly by the truths that we keep drinking in.

THE MORE WE ARE REGENERATED, THE MORE OUR SINS ARE LAID ASIDE

The more we are regenerated, the more our sins are laid aside, because the process of being regenerated is a matter of restraining our flesh so that it does not control us, and taming our old self and its cravings so that it does not rise up and destroy our intellectual faculty. Once our intellectual faculty is destroyed we can no longer be reformed; this reformation cannot take place unless our spirit, which is above our flesh, is instructed and perfected.

Surely everyone (whose intellect is still intact) can see from what was just stated that this sort of process cannot be completed in a moment. It happens in stages, much the way we are conceived, carried in the womb, born, and brought up, as was presented above. The traits of the flesh or the old self are embedded in us from the day we are born. They build the first home for our mind. Cravings live in that home like predatory animals in their dens. At first they live in the entryways. Then bit by bit they move by stealth into levels of the house that are below ground. Later on they go upstairs and make bedrooms for themselves there. This takes place gradually as we grow up from our childhood through youth to young adulthood, when we begin to have thoughts that come from our own understanding and perform actions that come from our own will.

Surely everyone can see that the home that has been established in our mind to this point—a place where cravings join hands and dance with each other like owls, vultures, and satyrs [Isaiah 13:21; 34:13–15]—cannot be torn down in a single moment and a new home constructed in its place. First the cravings that are holding hands and dancing have to be set to one side, and new healthy desires for what is good and true need to be brought in to replace our unhealthy desires for what is evil and false.

All this cannot happen in a moment. Every wise person can see the truth of this just from the fact that each evil is composed of countless cravings. Every evil is like a piece of fruit that under its skin is full of worms with black heads and white bodies. There are a great number of such evils and they are joined to each other, like a spider's offspring when they first hatch out of its belly. Therefore unless one evil after another is taken away until their confederation is broken up, we cannot become a new person.

These things have been stated to support the point that the more we are regenerated, the more our sins are laid aside.

From the day we are born we have an inclination toward evils of every kind. Because of that inclination we yearn for these evils. If we have the freedom, we also do them. From birth, we long to control other people and to own what belongs to them. These two longings tear to pieces any love we might have for our neighbor. They induce us to hate anyone who opposes us; that hatred leads us to desire revenge; and that desire for revenge inwardly cherishes the idea of our opponent's death. The same forces also lead us to think it is perfectly acceptable to commit adultery, to take things by secret acts of thievery, and to slander people, which is bearing false witness. People who think these things are acceptable are atheists at heart. This is the nature we are born with. Clearly then, we are born a hell in miniature.

Nevertheless, unlike animals, we are born with inner levels of mind that are spiritual. We are born for heaven. Because our earthly or outer self is a hell in miniature, as just noted, it follows that heaven cannot be planted in that hell; that hell must be moved out of the way.

People who know how heaven and hell differ from each other and how the one is located in relation to the other are able to know how we are regenerated and what we are like afterward. To make this better understood to those who do not have this knowledge, I will briefly reveal the following.

All those who are in heaven turn their faces toward the Lord. All who are in hell turn their faces away from the Lord. Therefore when you look at hell from heaven, you see only the backs of the people there and the backs of their heads; in fact they also look upside down (like people on the far side of the earth) with their feet up and their heads down, even though they walk on their feet and turn their faces this way and that. It is the fact that the inner levels of their minds are turned in the opposite direction that makes them look this way. This may sound hard to believe, but I have seen it myself.

These experiences revealed to me how regeneration takes place. It happens in the same way that hell is relocated and sequestered from heaven. As I noted above, by our first nature—the nature we are born with—we are a hell in miniature. By our second nature, the nature we derive from our second birth, we are a heaven in miniature.

It follows from this that the evils within us are relocated and sequestered on an individual scale in the same way that hell is relocated and sequestered from heaven on a grand scale. As our evils are relocated, they turn away from the Lord and gradually turn themselves upside down. This happens step by step as heaven is implanted in us—that is, as we become a new person.

In the hope of shedding further light, I will add that every evil within us has a connection to people in hell who are involved in that same evil. On the other hand, every good thing within us has a connection to people in heaven who are involved in that same goodness.

From these points it can be seen that being forgiven for our sins is not a matter of their being completely washed away or eliminated from us, but of their being relocated and sequestered within us. It is also clear that every evil that we have actively made our own stays with us.

Because "forgiveness of sins" means that they are relocated and sequestered within us, it follows that we are withheld from our evil by the Lord and held in goodness. This is the benefit that regeneration gives us.

THE ROLE OF LEVELS IN REGENERATION

There are levels of love and wisdom, consequent levels of warmth and light, and also levels of atmosphere. Without a knowledge that there are levels, what they are and what they are like, what is to follow will be incomprehensible, since there are levels in everything that has been created; therefore they exist in every form. Consequently, I need to discuss levels [here].

We can tell clearly from the angels of the three heavens that there are levels of love and wisdom. Angels of the third heaven so surpass angels of the second heaven in love and wisdom, and these in turn so surpass angels of the farthest heaven, that they cannot live in the same place. Their levels of love and wisdom mark them off and separate them. This is why angels of the lower heavens cannot climb up to angels of the higher heavens, and why if they are allowed to climb up they do not see anyone or anything around them. The reason they do not see anyone is that the love and wisdom of the higher angels is on a higher level, a level beyond their perception. Every angel actually is her or his love and wisdom; and love together with wisdom is human in form because God, who is love itself and wisdom itself, is human.

Occasionally I have been allowed to see angels of the farthest heaven go up to angels of the third heaven. When they managed to get there, I heard them complain that they could not see anyone; and yet they were surrounded by angels. They were afterwards told that these angels had been invisible to them because they could not perceive their love and wisdom, and it is love and wisdom that give angels their human appearance.

It is even clearer that there are levels of love and wisdom if we compare angels' love and wisdom with our love and wisdom. It is generally acknowledged that the wisdom of angels is unutterable, relatively speaking. It is also incomprehensible to us when we are wrapped up in our earthly love. The reason it seems unutterable and incomprehensible is that it is on a higher level.

Since there are levels of love and wisdom, there are levels of warmth and light—warmth and light here meaning spiritual warmth and light as angels experience them in the heavens and as they exist for us in the deeper levels of our minds. This is because we do have a warmth of love and a light of wisdom like that of angels.

It is like this in the heavens. The quality and amount of angels' love determines the quality and amount of their warmth, and their wisdom similarly determines their light. This is because there is love in their warmth and wisdom in their light. The same holds true for us on earth, but with the difference that angels feel the warmth and see the light, while we do not, the reason being that we are focused on physical warmth and light; and as long as we are, we feel spiritual warmth only as a kind of pleasure of love and see spiritual light only as a kind of sense of what is true.

Since people know nothing about the spiritual warmth and light within them as long as they are focused on physical warmth and light, and since they can know about this only through experience offered by the spiritual world, I need first of all to talk about the warmth and light that surround angels and their heavens. This is the one and only way to shed some light on this matter.

However, the levels of spiritual warmth cannot be described on the basis of experience because the love to which spiritual warmth corresponds does not fit into the images of our thought. Still, the levels of spiritual light can be described because light does fit. It is actually an attribute of thought. On the basis of levels of light, we can understand levels of spiritual warmth, since warmth and light are on comparable levels.

As for the spiritual light that surrounds angels, I have been allowed to see this with my own eyes. For angels of the higher heavens, the light is so brilliant that it is indescribable, even by comparison with the brilliance of snow; and it also has a glow that defies description, even by comparison with the radiant glory of our world's sun. In short, this light is a thousand times greater than the light at noon on earth. The light of angels of the lower heavens can in some measure be described by comparisons, though. Even so, it surpasses the highest level of light on earth.

The reason the light of angels of the higher heavens defies description is that this light is integral to their wisdom. Since their wisdom, relative to ours, is inexpressible, so is their light.

We can tell from these few facts that there are levels of light; and since wisdom and love occur on comparable levels, it follows that there are similar levels of warmth.

Since the atmospheres are what receive and hold warmth and light, it follows that there are as many levels of atmosphere as there are of warmth and light—as many, that is, as there are levels of love and wisdom. An abundance of experience in the spiritual world has shown me that there are several atmospheres, distinguished from each other by level. One kind of experience was especially convincing, namely that angels of lower heavens cannot breathe in the realm of higher angels. They seem to labor for breath like creatures taken out of the air into the ether, or like creatures taken out of the water into the air. Then too, the spirits below heaven look as though they were in a cloud.

There are two kinds of levels, vertical levels and horizontal levels. Knowing about levels is a kind of key to unlocking the causes of things and probing into them. In the absence of this knowledge, hardly anything can be known about causes. In the absence of this knowledge, the objects and subjects of both worlds look so simple that there seems to be nothing within them beyond what meets the eye. Actually, though, in comparison to what lies hidden within, this surface is like one feature compared to a thousand or ten thousand.

There is no way to uncover these deeper, invisible features without a knowledge of levels. We move from outer to inner and then to inmost by levels, and not by gradual levels but by distinct ones. "Gradual levels" is the name we give to declines or decreases from coarser to finer or denser to rarer, or better, to gains or increases from finer to coarser or from rarer to denser. They are just like going from light to darkness or from warmth to cold.

In contrast, distinct levels are totally different. They are like antecedent, subsequent, and final events, or like the purpose, the means, and the result. We refer to them as "distinct" because the antecedent event exists in its own right, the subsequent event in its own right, and the final event in its own right; and yet taken together they constitute a single whole.

Our atmospheres from top to bottom, from sun to earth, the atmospheres called ethers and airs, are marked off in levels of this kind. They are like the elements, compounds, and compounds of compounds that, taken all together, constitute a complex entity. These levels are distinct because they arise separately. They are what we mean by "vertical levels." The other levels, though, are gradual because they increase evenly. These are what we mean by "horizontal levels."

Absolutely everything that happens in the spiritual world and in the physical world results from a confluence of distinct and gradual levels, or of vertical and horizontal levels. We call the dimension constituted by distinct levels "height" and the dimension constituted by gradual levels "width." Their position relative to our eyesight does not change their labels.

Without a recognition of these levels, nothing can be known about the differences between the three heavens or about the differences of the love and wisdom of angels there, nothing about the differences of the warmth and light that surround them, nothing about the differences of the atmospheres that encompass and envelop them. Without a recognition of these levels, nothing can be known about differences of the inner abilities of our own minds, which means that nothing can be known about our states of reformation and regeneration, nothing about the differences of the outer, bodily abilities of both us and angels, nothing whatever about the difference between what is spiritual and what is physical and nothing therefore about correspondences, nothing about any difference between the life of humans and that of animals or between higher and lower animals, nothing about differences in the forms of the plant kingdom or the substances of the mineral kingdom.

We can tell from this that people who do not know about these levels do not see causes clearly and fairly. They see only effects and form judgments about causes on that basis—usually by tracing a string of effects. Yet causes produce effects not by simple continuity but by a distinct step. The cause is one thing and the effect another, and the difference between them is like the difference between an antecedent event and a subsequent one, or like the difference between what forms and what is formed.

The angelic heavens may serve as an example for better comprehension of the reality and nature of distinct levels and of how they differ from gradual levels. There are three heavens marked off by vertical levels so that one is underneath another. The only way they communicate is by an inflow that comes from the Lord through the heavens in sequence down to the lowest, and not the other way around.

Each heaven on its own, though, is marked off not by vertical levels but by horizontal ones. The people in the middle or center are in the light of wisdom, while those around them all the way to the borders are in the shadow of wisdom. That is, wisdom wanes all the way to ignorance as the light declines into shadow, which happens gradually.

It is the same with us. The inner realms of our minds are marked off into as many levels as are the angelic heavens, with one level over another. So the inner realms of our minds are marked off in distinct or vertical levels. This is why we can be engaged in the lowest level, a higher level, or the highest level depending on the level of our wisdom. It is why the higher level is closed when we are exclusively engaged in the lowest one, and why the higher one is opened as we accept wisdom from the Lord. There are also gradual or horizontal levels in us just as there are in heaven.

The reason we resemble the heavens is that we are miniature heavens as to the deeper realms of our minds when we are engaged in love and wisdom from the Lord. (On our being miniature heavens as to the deeper realms of our minds, see *Heaven and Hell* §§51–58.)

We can tell from this sample that people who know nothing about distinct or vertical levels cannot know anything about our state when it comes to reformation and regeneration, processes that are effected by our acceptance of love and wisdom from the Lord and a consequent opening of the deeper levels of our minds in due sequence. They cannot know, either, about the inflow through the heavens from the Lord or about the design into which they themselves were created. Anyone who ponders these subjects on the basis of gradual or horizontal levels rather than distinct or vertical ones can see them only in terms of effects and not at all in terms of causes. Seeing things solely in terms of effects is basing thought on illusions, which leads to one error after another. By inductive reasoning we can multiply these errors so much that ultimately grotesque distortions are labeled truths.

I am not aware that anything about distinct or vertical levels has yet come to people's attention—only things about gradual or horizontal levels. Yet nothing about causes can come to light in truth without familiarity with both kinds of level. That is why this whole part is devoted to this subject. . . .

Vertical levels are matched in kind, with one following from another in sequence like a purpose, a means, and a result. Since horizontal or gradual levels are like levels of light to shade, warmth to cold, hard to soft, dense to sparse, coarse to fine, and so on, and since we are familiar with these levels from our sensory and visual experience, while we are not familiar with vertical or distinct levels, I need to give particular attention to these latter in this part. Without familiarity with these levels, that is, we cannot see causes.

It is in fact recognized that a purpose, a means, and a result follow in sequence like antecedent, subsequent, and final events. It is recognized that the purpose produces the means and then produces the result through the means so that the purpose can be realized; and much more is recognized along the same lines. Knowing such things without seeing them by applying them to actual events, however, is only abstract knowledge. It lasts only as long as we are engaged in analytical thought on the basis of metaphysical principles. As a result, even though a purpose, a means, and a result do progress by distinct levels, still there is little if any knowledge of those levels in the world. Thinking only about abstractions is like something ethereal that dissipates; but if these abstract principles are applied to things of an earthly nature, then they are like something we see with our own eyes on earth, and they stay in our memory.

Everything in the world characterized by three dimensions, that is, everything we call a compound, is constituted by three vertical or distinct levels. Some examples may make this clear. We know from visual experience that every muscle in the human body is made up of tiny fibers and that these, gathered into bundles, make up the larger fibers we call motor fibers. From these bundles comes that compound entity called a muscle.

It is the same with our nerves. The smallest fibers in them are woven together into larger ones that look like threads, and gatherings of these are woven together into nerves. It is the same with the rest of the weavings, bundlings, and gatherings that make up our organs and viscera. They are compounds of fibers and vessels in various arrangements, depending on similar levels.

It is the same as well in all the members of the plant kingdom and all the members of the mineral kingdom. There are threefold gatherings of filaments in wood and threefold conglomerates of elements in metals and rocks as well.

We can see from this what distinct levels are like, namely that one level is made from another and a third from the second, the third being called a compound. Each level is distinct from the other.

On this basis we can draw conclusions about things not visible to our eyes, since their arrangement is similar—for example about the organized substances that are the vessels and dwellings of the thoughts and feelings in our brains, about the atmospheres, about warmth and light, and about love and wisdom. The atmospheres are vessels of warmth and light, and warmth and light are vessels of love and wisdom. So if there are levels of the atmospheres, then there are similar levels of warmth and light and similar levels of love and wisdom. There is not one set of relationships in one case and a different set in another.

We can tell from what has just been said that these levels are consistent, of the same character and nature. The smallest, larger, and largest motor fibers of our muscles have the same basic nature. The smallest, larger, and largest nerve fibers match; the woody filaments match from their smallest forms to their compounds; and the parts of rocks and metals match in the same way. The organized substances that are vessels and dwellings of our thoughts and feelings match, from the very simplest to their overall compound, the brain. The atmospheres match, from pure ether to air. The levels of warmth and light that parallel those of the atmospheres in their sequence match; and therefore so do the levels of love and wisdom.

Things that are not of the same character and nature do not match and do not harmonize with things that do. This means that they cannot combine with them to make up distinct levels. They can combine only with their own kind, with things of the same character and nature, things that match.

Clearly, these levels are in a sequence like that of a purpose, a means, and a result, since the first or smallest promotes its cause through the intermediate and achieves its result through the last.

It is important to realize that each level is delineated from the other by its own membrane, with all the levels together being delineated by a common membrane. This common membrane communicates with the deeper and deepest levels in proper sequence, which is what makes possible the union and concerted action of all of them. . . .

In a sequential arrangement, the first level is the highest and the third the lowest, while in a simultaneous arrangement, the first level is the center and the third level is the circumference. There is a sequential arrangement and a simultaneous one. The sequential arrangement of these levels is from highest to lowest or from top to bottom. This is the arrangement of the angelic heavens, with the third heaven as the highest, the second in between, and the first as the lowest. These are their relative locations.

The same sequential arrangement applies to states of love and wisdom among angels in heaven, to warmth and light, and to spiritual atmospheres. The same arrangement applies to all the processes of perfection of events and forms there.

When the vertical or distinct levels are in this sequential arrangement, they are like a tower divided into three floors so that one can go up or down. The most perfect and lovely things are on the top floor, less perfect and lovely things on the middle floor, and still less perfect and lovely things on the lowest floor.

In a simultaneous arrangement of the same levels, though, it looks different. Then the highest elements of the sequential arrangement—as I have mentioned, the most perfect and lovely ones—are in the center, the lower ones in an intermediate region, and the lowest on the outside. It is as though there were a solid object made up of these three levels with the finest substances in the middle or center, less fine particles around that, and on the outside, forming a kind of envelope, parts composed of these and therefore coarsest. It is as though the tower we were talking about had settled into a plane, with the top floor becoming the center, the middle floor an intermediate region, and the lowest floor the outside.

Since the highest thing in sequential arrangement is the central thing in simultaneous arrangement and the lowest is the outermost, "higher" in the Word means more internal and "lower" means more external. The same holds for "upward" and "downward" and for "high" and "low."

In every final form there are distinct levels in simultaneous arrangement. This is the arrangement of the motor fibers in every muscle, the fibers in every nerve, the fibers and tiny vessels in all our viscera and organs. At the heart of each are the simplest and most perfect substances, while the outside is formed from their compounds.

The same arrangement of these levels is found in every seed, every fruit, even in every metal and rock. This is the nature of the parts that constitute their totality. Their central, intermediate, and outermost parts are on these levels, and they themselves are successive compounds, aggregates, or masses of these simple components that are their primary substances and materials.

In short, there are levels like this in every final form and therefore in every effect, since every final form consists of antecedents that in turn consist of things primary to them. Likewise every result comes from a means and every means from a purpose, the purpose being the whole essence of the means and the means the whole essence of the result, as I have just explained. Further, the purpose constitutes the center, the means the intermediate, and the result the final outcome.

The same holds for levels of love and wisdom, warmth and light, and for the organized forms of feelings and thoughts within us. I have discussed the sequence of these levels in sequential and simultaneous arrangements in *Sacred Scripture* §38 and elsewhere, showing that there are similar levels in all the details of the Word.

The final level is the composite, vessel, and foundation of the prior levels. Examples of the principle of levels that is under discussion in this part have thus far been drawn from various things that occur in our two worlds—levels of the heavens where angels live, for example, levels of the warmth and light that surround them, of the atmospheres, of various parts of the human body, and of things in the animal and mineral kingdoms. The principle of levels has a wider range, though. Its range includes not only physical phenomena but also societal, moral, and spiritual ones in all their detail.

There are two reasons why the principle of levels includes such matters. The first is that there is a trine in everything that can be said to have attributes, a trine called purpose, means, and result; and these three are related to each other by vertical levels. The second reason is that no societal, moral, or spiritual phenomenon is abstract or disembodied. They are matters of substance, for just as love and wisdom are not abstractions but substances, so are all the things we refer to as societal, moral, and spiritual. We can of course think about them in the abstract, as disembodied, but in their own right they are not abstractions. Take feeling and thought, for example, or goodwill and faith, or will and understanding. What applies to love and wisdom applies to them as well, namely that they do not happen apart from subjects that are substantial. They actually have to do with the state of those subjects or substances. They are shifts of state that give rise to change. "Substance" means form as well, since there is no such thing as a formless substance.

Since we can think about will and understanding, about feeling and thought, and about goodwill and faith apart from the substantial realities that are their subjects, and since we have thought about them in this way, we have lost any appropriate concept of them, any realization that they refer to the states of substantial realities or forms. Exactly the same principle applies to sensations and actions, which are not things in the abstract apart from our sensory and motor organs. In the abstract, or apart from their organs, they are theoretical constructs only. They are like sight with no eye, hearing with no ear, taste with no tongue, and so on.

Since all societal, moral, and spiritual events, like all physical ones, happen not only by gradual levels but also on distinct levels, and since processes on distinct levels are like the processes of purpose to means and means to result, I should like to illustrate and demonstrate the present topic (that the final level is the composite, vessel, and foundation of the prior levels) by what I have just mentioned, namely instances of love and wisdom, of will and understanding, of feeling and thought, and of goodwill and faith.

We can tell quite clearly that the final level is the composite, vessel, and foundation of the prior ones by looking at the way purpose and means progress to result. Enlightened reason can grasp the fact that the effect is the composite, vessel, and foundation of the means and the purpose, but cannot grasp as clearly the fact that the purpose in all fullness and the means in all fullness are actively present in the result, with the result being completely inclusive of them.

This follows from what has already been said in this part, especially from the fact that one level comes from another in a three-stage sequence and that a result is simply a purpose in its final form. Since the final form is this kind of composite, it follows that the final form is their vessel and also their foundation.

As for love and wisdom, love is the purpose, wisdom the means, and service the result. Further, service is the composite, vessel, and foundation of wisdom and love, such a composite and such a vessel that every bit of love and every bit of wisdom is actively present in it. It is their total presence. We need to be absolutely clear, though, that what are present in service are all the elements of love and wisdom that are of the same kind, harmonious.

Desire, thought, and act occur on a sequence of similar levels, since every desire has to do with love, every thought with wisdom, and every act with service. Goodwill, faith, and good works occur on the same sequence of levels, since goodwill is a matter of desire, faith of thought, and good works of act. Will, understanding, and practice occur on the same sequence of levels as well, since will is a matter of love and therefore of desire, understanding of wisdom and therefore of faith, and practice of service and therefore of deeds. Just as all the elements of wisdom and love dwell within service, all the elements of thought and desire dwell within act, and all the elements of faith and goodwill dwell within deeds, and so on. This means all the elements that are of the same kind; that is, they are harmonious.

People have not yet recognized that the last member of each sequence—service, act, deed, and practice—is the composite and vessel of all the earlier members. It seems as though there were nothing more within service, act, deed, or practice than there is within motion. However, all these prior stages are actively present within, so completely present that nothing is missing. They are enclosed within it the way wine is enclosed in a bottle or furnishings in a house.

The reason this is not noticed is that we look at acts of service from the outside only, and things seen from the outside are simply events and motions. It is like seeing our arms and hands move and not knowing that a thousand motor fibers are cooperating in each movement, with a thousand elements of thought and desire answering to those thousand motor fibers and stimulating them. Since these things are happening far inside, they are not visible to any of our physical senses. This much is known, that nothing is done in or through the body except from will and through thought; and since these two are acting, every element of will and thought must necessarily be present within the act. They cannot be separated. This is why we draw conclusions on the basis of deeds or works about each other's purposeful thought, which we refer to as "intent."

I have learned that angels can sense and see from someone's single deed or work everything about the intention and thought of the one who is doing it. From the person's will, angels of the third heaven see the purpose for which it is being done, and angels of the second heaven see the means through which the purpose is working. This is why deeds and works are so often mandated in the Word, and why it says that we are known by our works.

According to angelic wisdom, unless will and understanding, or desire and thought, or goodwill and faith, devote themselves to involvement in works or deeds whenever possible, they are nothing but passing breezes, so to speak, or images in the air that vanish. They first take on permanence in us and become part of our life when we perform and do them. The reason is that the final stage is the composite, vessel, and foundation of the prior stages.

Faith apart from good works is just this kind of airy nothing or image, and so are faith and goodwill apart from their practice. The only difference is that people who put faith and goodwill together know what is good and are able to intend and do it, but not people who are devoted to faith apart from goodwill. . . .

These three vertical levels exist in each of us from birth and can be opened in sequence. As they are opened, we are in the Lord and the Lord is in us. The existence of three vertical levels in us has not been widely recognized before. This is because vertical levels themselves have not been identified, and as long as these levels have been unrecognized, the only levels people could know about are the gradual ones. When these are the only levels people know about, they can believe that our love and wisdom increase only gradually.

It needs to be realized, though, that we all have these three vertical or distinct levels in us from our birth, one above or within the other, and that each vertical or distinct level has horizontal or gradual levels by which it increases incrementally. This is because there are both kinds of level in everything, no matter how large or small. Neither kind of level can exist apart from the other.

These three vertical levels are called earthly, spiritual, and heavenly. When we are born, we come first into the earthly level, which gradually develops within us in keeping with the things we learn and the intelligence we gain through this learning, all the way to that summit of intelligence called rationality. This by itself, though, does not open the second level, the one called spiritual. This level is opened by a love for being useful that comes from our intelligence; but the love for being useful is a spiritual one, a love for our neighbor.

In the same way, this level can develop by incremental steps all the way to its summit; and it does so by our discovering what is true and good, or by spiritual truths. Even so, these do not open that third level that is called heavenly. This is opened by a heavenly love for being useful that is a love for the Lord; and love for the Lord is nothing but applying the precepts of the Word to our lives, these precepts being essentially to abstain from evil things because they are hellish and demonic and to do good things because they are heavenly and divine. This is how the three levels are opened in us sequentially.

As long as we are living in this world, we have no knowledge of any opening of levels within us. This is because our attention is focused on the earthly level, which is the most remote. We are thinking, intending, and talking and acting on that basis; and the spiritual level, which is deeper, does not communicate with the earthly level directly, but only by correspondence. Communication by correspondence is imperceptible.

However, as soon as we put off the earthly level, which happens when we die, we come into awareness of whatever level has been opened within us in the world, of the spiritual level if that level has been opened, of the heavenly level if that level has been opened. If we become conscious on the spiritual level after death, then we no longer think, intend, or talk or act in an earthly way, but spiritually. If we become conscious on the heavenly level, then we think, intend, and talk and act on that level. Further, since communication among the three levels occurs only by correspondence, the differences in level of love, wisdom, and useful function are so definite that there is no communication between them by direct contact.

We can see from this that we do have three vertical levels and that these can be opened in sequence.

Because there are within us these three levels of love and wisdom and therefore of usefulness, it follows that there are three levels of will and understanding and consequent closure, and therefore of concentration within us on usefulness, since will is the vessel of love, understanding the vessel of wisdom, and closure the usefulness that results from them. We can see from this that there are within each of us an earthly, a spiritual, and a heavenly will and understanding, potentially at birth, and effectively at the point when they are opened.

In short, the human mind, consisting of will and understanding, has three levels from creation and birth, so we have an earthly mind, a spiritual mind, and a heavenly mind. Consequently, we can be raised into angelic wisdom and possess it even while we are living in this world. Still, we become conscious of it only after death, if we become angels; and then we say inexpressible things, things incomprehensible to an earthly-minded person.

I was acquainted with a moderately educated man in the world and saw him and talked with him in heaven after his death. I sensed very clearly that he was talking like an angel and that what he was saying was beyond the grasp of earthly-minded people. The reason was that in the world he had applied the precepts of the Word to his life and had worshiped the Lord; so the Lord had raised him into the third level of love and wisdom.

It is important to know about this raising up of the human mind, since understanding what follows depends on it.

There are two abilities within us, gifts from the Lord, that distinguish us from animals. One ability is that we can discern what is true and what is good. This ability is called "rationality," and is an ability of our understanding. The other ability is that we can do what is true and what is good. This ability is called "freedom," and is an ability of our will. Because of our rationality, we can think what we want to think, either in favor of God or against God, in favor of our neighbor or against our neighbor. We can also intend and do what we are thinking, or when we see something evil and are afraid of the penalty, can use our freedom to refrain from doing it. It is because of these two abilities that we are human and are distinguished from animals.

These two abilities are gifts from the Lord within us. They come from him constantly and are never taken away, for if they were taken away, that would be the end of our humanity. The Lord lives in each of us, in the good and the evil alike, in these two abilities. They are the Lord's dwelling in the human race, which is why everyone, whether good or evil, lives forever. However, the Lord's dwelling within us is more intimate as we use these abilities to open the higher levels. By opening them, we come into consciousness of higher levels of love and wisdom and so come closer to the Lord. It makes sense, then, that as these levels are opened, we are in the Lord and the Lord is in us.

I have noted above that the three vertical levels are like a purpose, a means, and a result, and that the sequence of love, wisdom, and usefulness follows this sequence. I need at this point, then, to say a little about love as the purpose, wisdom as the means, and usefulness as the result.

People who pay attention to their reason when that reason is in the light can see that our love is the purpose of everything we do, since it is what we love that we think about, decide upon, and do, so it is what we have as our purpose. Our reason can also show us that wisdom is the means, since the love that is our purpose gathers in our understanding the means it needs to reach its goal. So it listens to its wisdom, and these resources constitute the means through which it works. We can see without further explanation that usefulness is the result.

Love, though, is not the same in one individual as in another, so wisdom is not the same in one individual as in another, and neither is usefulness. Since these three are matched in kind, the quality of our love determines the quality of our wisdom, and of our usefulness. I say "wisdom," but this means whatever is characteristic of our understanding.

Spiritual light flows in within us through three levels, but not spiritual warmth except to the extent that we abstain from evils as sins and turn to the Lord. Light and warmth emanate from the sun of heaven, that sun that is the first emanation of divine love and wisdom [the Lord]. The light emanates from his wisdom and the warmth from his love. Further, the light is the vessel of wisdom and the warmth is the vessel of love; and the more we are engaged in wisdom, the more we come into that divine light, and the more we are engaged in love, the more we come into that divine warmth.

We can also tell from what has been presented that there are three levels of light and three levels of warmth, or three levels of wisdom and three levels of love, and that these levels are formed within us in such a way that we are open to divine love and wisdom and therefore to the Lord.

The present task, then, is to show that while spiritual light flows in through these three levels in us, spiritual warmth does not—except to the extent that we abstain from evils as sins and turn to the Lord; or what amounts to the same thing, to show that we can accept wisdom all the way to the third level, but not love—unless we abstain from evils as sins and turn to the Lord; or (what again amounts to the same thing) to show that our understanding can be raised up into wisdom, but our will cannot be raised up [into love]—except to the extent that we abstain from evils as sins.

It has become abundantly clear to me from my experiences in the spiritual world that our understanding can be raised up into heaven's light, or into angelic wisdom, but that our will cannot be raised up into heaven's warmth or angelic love unless we abstain from evils as sins and turn to the Lord. I have often seen and sensed that very ordinary spirits who knew only that God exists and that the Lord was born as a human—hardly anything else—understood the mysteries of angelic wisdom completely, almost the way angels do. Nor were they the only ones. Even many members of the demonic mob understood. They understood while they were listening, that is, but not in their private thinking. When they were listening, light flowed into them from above; but in their private thinking the only light that could get in was the light that agreed with their warmth or love. So even after they had heard these mysteries and grasped them, when they turned their hearing away they retained nothing. In fact, the members of the devil's mob spat it out and denied it categorically. The reason was that the fire of their love and its light, being mindless, brought down a darkness that snuffed out the heavenly light that was flowing in from above.

It is the same in this world. Anyone who has any sense at all and has not become inwardly convinced of false principles on the grounds of intellectual pride, on hearing people talk about higher things or on reading about them understands, retains them, and eventually affirms them if there is any desire for learning. This holds true for evil and good people alike. Even evil people who at heart deny the divine gifts of the church can understand, discuss, and preach higher things, and can defend them in scholarly writing. However, when they are left on their own to think about them, their thinking is based on their hellish self-centeredness, and they deny them. We can see from this that our understanding can be in spiritual light even though our will may not be in spiritual warmth.

It also follows from this that our understanding does not lead our will, or that wisdom does not give rise to love. It merely teaches and shows the way. It teaches how we should live and shows us the way we should follow. It also follows from this that our will leads our understanding and gets it to work in unison with itself. The love that is the substance of our will gives the name of "wisdom" to whatever in our understanding it finds harmonious.

On its own, apart from understanding, our will accomplishes nothing. Everything it does, it does in conjunction with our understanding. However, our will gains the cooperation of our understanding by flowing into it, and not the other way around.

Now I need to describe how light flows into the three levels that make up the human mind. From our birth, the forms that are receptive of warmth and light or love and wisdom (which are in a threefold pattern or on three levels) are translucent and let spiritual light pass through, the way clear glass lets physical light through. This is why we can be raised up all the way to the third level in respect to our wisdom. These forms are not opened, though, until spiritual warmth, or the love of wisdom, is united to the spiritual light. It is through this union that the translucent forms are opened level by level.

This is like the light and warmth of the world's sun and plant life on earth. The winter light is just as bright as summer light, but it does not open anything in seeds or trees. However, when the warmth of spring is united to that light then things open. The resemblance stems from the fact that spiritual light is analogous to physical light and spiritual warmth is analogous to physical warmth.

The only way to gain that spiritual warmth is by abstaining from evils as sins and then turning to the Lord, since as long as we are caught up in evil pursuits we are caught up in a love for them. We are enmeshed in our cravings for them; and that love for what is evil, that craving, is a form of love that is opposed to spiritual love and desire. Further, the only way to get rid of that love or craving is by abstaining from evils as sins; and since we cannot do that on our own, but only by the Lord's agency, we need to turn to him. When we do abstain from our evils by the Lord's agency, then, our love for evil and its warmth are put aside and a love for what is good, with its warmth, is brought in in its place, enabling a higher level to be opened. The Lord actually flows in from above and opens it and unites the love or spiritual warmth with wisdom or spiritual light. As a result of this union we begin to blossom spiritually like a tree in springtime.

We are differentiated from animals by the inflow of spiritual light into all three levels of our minds; and beyond what animals can do, we can think analytically; we can see things that are true not only on the earthly level but on the spiritual level as well; and when we see them, we can acknowledge them and so be reformed and regenerated. Our ability to accept spiritual light is what we call rationality, already discussed. It is a gift from the Lord to each one of us, and one that is not taken away, since if it were taken away, we could not be reformed. It is because of this ability called rationality that we not only can think but can say what we are thinking, which animals cannot do. Then because of that second ability called freedom, also discussed above, we can do what we have thought intellectually.

If that higher level, the spiritual level, is not opened in us, we become focused on the physical world and our sense impressions. I have just explained that there are three levels of the human mind called earthly, spiritual, and heavenly; that these levels can be opened in us in sequence; that the earthly level is opened first; and that afterward, if we abstain from evils as sins and turn to the Lord, the spiritual level is opened, and ultimately the heavenly level. Since the sequential opening of these levels depends on how we live, it follows that the two higher levels may also not be opened, in which case we stay on the earthly level, which is the most remote.

It is recognized in the world that we have an earthly self and a spiritual self, or an outer and an inner self. It is not recognized that the earthly self becomes spiritual by the opening of a higher level within, and that this opening is accomplished by a spiritual life, a life in accord with divine precepts, and that unless we live by these precepts, we remain centered on the physical world.

There are three kinds of earthly-minded people. One kind is made up of individuals who have no knowledge of divine precepts, a second of people who know that such precepts exist but give no thought to living by them, and a third of people who trivialize and deny them. As for the first kind, the ones who have no knowledge of divine precepts, they cannot help remaining earthly-minded because there is no way for them to teach themselves. We all learn about divine precepts from others, who know about them from their religion. We do not gain them by direct revelation (see *Sacred Scripture* §§114–118).

People of the second kind, the ones who know that divine precepts exist but give no thought to living by them, also remain earthly-minded and are not concerned with anything except what is worldly and physical. After death they become employees and servants of the spiritual-minded, performing for them the functions for which they are fitted. This is because an earthly-minded individual is an employee or servant, while a spiritual-minded one is an employer or householder.

People of the third kind, the ones who trivialize and deny divine precepts, not only remain earthly-minded but even become sense-centered to the extent that they trivialize and deny divine precepts. Sense-centered people are the lowest of the earthly-minded, unable to raise their thoughts above deceptive physical appearances. After death, they are in hell.

Since people in this world do not know what a spiritual-minded person is and what an earthly-minded person is, and since many call someone "spiritual" who is merely earthly-minded, and vice versa, I need to say the following things clearly.

1. What an earthly-minded person is and what a spiritual-minded person is.

2. What an earthly-minded person is like whose spiritual level has been opened.

3. What an earthly-minded person is like whose spiritual level has not been opened but is not yet closed.

4. What an earthly-minded person is like whose spiritual level has been completely closed.

5. Lastly, the difference between the life of a wholly earthly minded person and the life of an animal.

1. *What an earthly-minded person is and what a spiritual-minded person is.* We are not human because of our faces and bodies but

because of our power to understand and our power to will, so "earthly-minded person" and "spiritual-minded person" refer to our understanding and will, which can be either earthly or spiritual. When we are earthly-minded, we are like an earthly world in respect to our understanding and will and can even be called a world or microcosm. When we are spiritual-minded, we are like a spiritual world in respect to our understanding and will, and can even be called a spiritual world or a heaven.

We can see from this that earthly-minded people, being a kind of image of the earthly world, love whatever has to do with the earthly world, while spiritual-minded people, being a kind of image of the spiritual world, love whatever has to do with that world or heaven. Spiritual-minded people do love the earthly world, it is true, but only the way householders love their servants, who enable them to be of service. In fact, the earthly-minded people become spiritual in a way through their service. This happens when an earthly-minded person feels the joy of service from a spiritual source. This kind of earthly-minded person is called "earthly-spiritual."

Spiritual-minded people love spiritual truths, not only loving to know and understand them but intending them as well; while earthly-minded people love to talk about these truths and carry them out as well. Putting truths into action is being of service. This ranking comes from the way the spiritual world and the earthly world go together, since anything that surfaces and exists in the earthly world has its cause in the spiritual world.

We can tell from this that spiritual-minded people are completely distinct from earthly-minded people, and that the only communication between them is the kind that occurs between a cause and its effect.

2. *What an earthly-minded person is like whose spiritual level has been opened.* This you can see from what has already been said; but I need to add that an earthly-minded person is a complete person

when the spiritual level has been opened within. Once that happens, we are actually in the company of angels in heaven at the same time that we are in the company of people on earth, living under the watchful care of the Lord in both realms. Spiritual-minded people derive their imperatives from the Lord through the Word and carry them out by means of their earthly selves.

Earthly-minded individuals whose spiritual level has been opened do not realize that they are thinking and acting from their spiritual selves. They seem to themselves to be acting on their own, though in fact it is not on their own but from the Lord. Earthly-minded people whose spiritual level has been opened do not realize that they are in heaven because of their spiritual selves, either, even though their spiritual selves are surrounded by heaven's angels. Sometimes such people are even visible to angels, but since they are drawn back to their earthly selves, they vanish in a little while.

Earthly people whose spiritual level has been opened do not realize that their spiritual minds are filled with thousands of hidden treasures of wisdom and with thousands of love's joys as gifts from the Lord. They do not realize that they will begin to participate in this wisdom and joy after they die, when they become angels. The reason earthly-minded people are not aware of all this is that communication between our earthly and our spiritual selves takes place by correspondences, and communication by correspondences is perceived in our understanding only as seeing truths in the light, and in our will only as being helpful because we enjoy it.

3. *What an earthly-minded person is like whose spiritual level has not been opened but is not yet closed.* The spiritual level is not opened in us but is still not closed when we are leading a life that involves some goodwill but do not know very much real truth. This is because that level is opened by a union of love and wisdom, or of warmth and light. Love alone, or spiritual warmth alone, will not do it, and neither will wisdom alone or spiritual light alone.

It takes both together. So if we do not know the real truths that constitute wisdom or light, love cannot manage to open that level. All it can do is keep it able to be opened, which is what "not being closed" means. The same holds true for plant life. Warmth alone will not make seeds sprout or trees leaf out. Warmth together with light is what does it.

We need to realize that everything true is a matter of spiritual light and that everything good is a matter of spiritual warmth, and that what is good opens the spiritual level by means of true things, since goodness does what is helpful by means of truths. Helpful acts are the good that love does, deriving their essence from the union of what is good and what is true.

What happens after death to people whose spiritual level is not opened but still not closed is that since they are still earthly-minded and not spiritual-minded, they are in the lowest parts of heaven, where they sometimes have a hard time of it. Alternatively, they may be around the edges of a somewhat higher heaven, where they live in a kind of twilight. This is because in heaven and in each distinct community the light decreases from the center to the circumference, and the people who are especially engaged with divine truths are in the middle, while the people who are only slightly engaged in truths are at the borders. People are only slightly engaged with truths if all they have learned from their religion is that God exists, that the Lord suffered for their sake, and that goodwill and faith are the essential qualities of the church, without making any effort to find out what faith is and what goodwill is. Yet essentially, faith is truth, and truth is complex, while goodwill can be defined as every duty we fulfill because of the Lord. We do things because of the Lord when we abstain from evils as sins.

This is just what I have already said. The purpose is the whole substance of the means, and the purpose through the means is the whole substance of the result. The purpose is thoughtful action, or some good, the means is faith, or something true, and the results are good deeds or acts of service. We can see from this that nothing of goodwill can be instilled into our deeds except to the extent that our goodwill is united to those truths that we attribute to faith. They are the means by which goodwill enters into works and gives them their quality.

4. *What an earthly-minded person is like whose spiritual level has been completely closed.* The spiritual level is closed in people who are focused on evil in their lives, especially if they are engaged in distortion because of their evils. It is rather like the way our little nerve fibers contract at the slightest touch of anything unsuitable, as does every muscular motor fiber and every muscle and the whole body, at the touch of something hard or cold. This is how the substances or forms of the spiritual level within us react to things that are evil and to the distortions that result—they are unsuitable. The spiritual level, being in the form of heaven, is open only to things that are good and to the truths that result from what is good. These are congenial to it, while evils and the falsities they give rise to are unsuitable.

This level contracts, and closes by contracting, especially in people who are caught up in a love of being in control for selfish reasons in this world, since this love is the opposite of a love for the Lord. It is also closed, though not as firmly, in people who because of their love for this world are caught up in a mindless craving to acquire the assets of others. The reason these loves close off the spiritual level is that they are the sources of our evils.

The contraction or closure of this level is like a coil twisting back on itself, which is why this level deflects heaven's light once it has been closed. This yields darkness in place of heaven's light. Accordingly, the truth that is found in heaven's light becomes sickening.

For these people, it is not just [the spiritual] level itself that is closed. It is also the higher area of the earthly level, the area called "rational." Eventually, then, only the lowest area of the earthly level stays open, the area we call "sensory." This is right next to the world and to our outward physical senses, which thereafter constitute the basis of our thinking, talking, and rationalizing. In the spiritual world, earthly-minded people who have become sense-centered because of their evils and consequent distortions do not look human in heaven's light. They look grotesque, with flattened noses. The reason they have these concave noses is that the nose corresponds to a perception of what is true. They cannot bear a single ray of heaven's light, either. The only light in their caves is like the light of embers or smoldering charcoal. We can see from this who the people are whose spiritual level has been closed, and what they are like.

5. *The difference between the life of an earthly-minded person and the life of an animal.* I need to deal with this difference more specifically later. At this point I need to say only that we humans differ in having three levels of mind or three levels of understanding and will, and that these levels can be opened in sequence. Since they are translucent, we can be raised in understanding into heaven's light and see things that are not only civically and morally true but spiritually true as well. Once we have seen many such truths, we can on that basis draw a series of true conclusions, and keep perfecting our understanding in this way forever.

Animals, though, do not have the two higher levels, only the earthly levels, and apart from the higher levels the earthly levels have no ability to think about any civic, moral, or spiritual issue. Further, since these earthly levels cannot be opened and therefore raised into higher light, animals cannot think in sequential order. They can think only in a simultaneous pattern, and that is not really thinking. It is simply acting on the basis of the knowledge that answers to their love; and since they cannot think analytically or survey their lower thought from any higher vantage point, they cannot talk. All they can do is make sounds that suit their love's knowledge.

The only difference between sense-centered people (the lowest of the earthly-minded) and animals is that they can fill their minds with information and think and talk on that basis. They get this from an ability we all possess, our ability to understand what is true if we want to. This ability makes the difference. However, many people have made themselves lower than animals by their abuse of this ability.

In its own right, the earthly level of the human mind is a continuum, but because of its responsiveness to the two higher levels, it seems to have distinct levels when it is raised up. Even though it is hard for people to understand this if they are not yet familiar with vertical levels, it still needs to be disclosed, since it is a matter of angelic wisdom. While earthly-minded people cannot think about this wisdom the way angels do, they can still grasp it mentally if their minds are raised into the level of light that angels enjoy. Our minds can actually be raised that far and enlightened accordingly. However, this enlightenment of our earthly minds does not happen by distinct levels. There is instead a gradual increase, and in keeping with that increase, our minds are enlightened from within, with the light of the two higher levels.

We can understand how this happens by perceiving that for vertical levels, one is above the other, with the earthly level, the terminal one, acting like an inclusive membrane for the two higher levels. As the earthly level is raised toward a higher level, then, the higher activates that outer earthly level from within and enlightens it. The enlightenment is actually happening because of the light of the higher levels from within, but it is received gradually by the earthly level that envelops and surrounds them, with greater clarity and purity as it ascends. That is, the earthly level is enlightened from within, from the light of the higher, distinct levels; but on the earthly level itself, it happens gradually.

We can see from this that as long as we are in this world and are therefore focused on the earthly level, we cannot be raised into wisdom itself, the way it is for angels. We can be raised only into a higher light at the boundary of angels and receive enlightenment from their light, which flows into us from within and illumines us.

I cannot describe this any more clearly. It is better understood through its effects; for if we have some prior knowledge about causes, their effects embody and present them in the light and thereby make them clear.

The following are "effects." (a) Our earthly mind can be raised as far as the light of heaven that surrounds angels, and can therefore sense on the earthly level what angels sense spiritually—that is, it does not sense so fully. Still, our earthly mind cannot be raised all the way into angelic light itself. (b) With our earthly mind raised as far as heaven's light, we can think and even talk with angels; but when this happens, the thought and speech of the angels are flowing into our earthly thought and speech, and not the other way around. This means that angels talk with us in earthly language, in our native tongues. (c) This happens by a flow of the spiritual level into the earthly, and not by any flow of the earthly level into the spiritual. (d) There is no way for our human wisdom, which is earthly as long as we are living in the earthly world, to be raised into angelic wisdom, only into some reflection of it. This is because the raising of the earthly mind is along a continuum, like that of darkness to light, or coarse to fine. Still, if our spiritual level has been opened, we come into consciousness of that wisdom when we die, and we can also come into consciousness of it through the quiescence of our physical senses, and then through an inflow from above into the spiritual elements of our minds. (e) Our earthly mind is made up of both spiritual substances and earthly substances. Our thinking results from the spiritual substances and not from the earthly substances. These latter substances fade away when we die, but the spiritual substances do not. So when we become spirits or angels after death, the same mind is still there in the form it had in the world. (f) The earthly substances of our minds (which fade away after death, as I have just noted) form the skin-like covering of the spiritual bodies we inhabit as spirits and angels. It is by means of this covering, taken from the earthly world, that our spiritual bodies have their stability, the earthly substance being the outermost vessel. This is why there is no angel or spirit who was not born human.

These hidden treasures of angelic wisdom are appended at this point to show the nature of our earthly mind.

Each of us is born with the ability to understand truths even at the deepest level where angels of the third heaven live. As our human understanding climbs up on a continuum around the two higher levels, it receives the light of wisdom from those levels in the manner already described. As a result, we can become rational in proportion to its ascent. If it comes up to the third level, it becomes rational from the third level; if it comes up to the second level, it becomes rational from the second level; and if it does not ascend at all, it is rational on the first level. We say that it becomes rational from those levels because the earthly level is the general recipient vessel of their light.

The reason we do not become rational to the highest degree we are capable of is that our love, which is a matter of our will, cannot be raised up in the same way as our wisdom, which is a matter of our understanding. The love that is a matter of will is raised only by abstaining from evils as sins and then by those good actions of thoughtfulness that are acts of service, acts that we are then performing from the Lord. So if the love that is a matter of will is not raised up along with it, then no matter how high the wisdom that is a matter of our understanding has risen, it ultimately falls back to the level of its love. This is why we become rational only on the lowest level if our love is not raised to the spiritual level as well.

We can tell from all this that our rational ability seems to be made up of three levels, one ability from the heavenly level, one from the spiritual level, and one from the earthly level. We can also tell that our rationality, an ability that can be raised, is still with us whether it is raised up or not.

I have stated that everyone is born with this ability, or with rationality, but this means everyone whose outward organs have not been damaged by any external events in the womb, or after birth by illness or some head injury, or by the outburst of a senseless love that lowers all restraints. The rational ability cannot be raised up for people like this. The life of their will and understanding has no boundaries in which it finds definition, that is, boundaries so arranged that the life can accomplish outward deeds coherently. It does act in keeping with outermost boundaries, but not because of them.

The earthly mind, being the envelope and vessel of the higher levels of the human mind, is reactive. If the higher levels are not opened, it acts against them; whereas if they are opened, it acts with them. I explained in the last section that since the earthly mind is on the last level, it surrounds and encloses the spiritual mind and the heavenly mind, which are on higher levels. Now we have reached the point where I need to show that the earthly mind reacts against the higher or inner minds. The reason it reacts is that it does surround, enclose, and contain them. This could not happen without that reaction, since if it did not react, the enclosed inner elements would start to spread and force their way out so that they dissipated. It would be as though the coverings of the human body were not reacting, in which case the viscera within the body would spill out and trickle away; or it would be as though the membranes around the motor fibers of our muscles did not react against the forces of those fibers when they were activated. Not only would the action cease, the whole inner web-like structure would unravel as well.

It is the same with any terminal vertical level. So it is the same with the earthly mind relative to the higher levels, since as I have just said, there are three levels of the human mind, earthly, spiritual, and heavenly, and the earthly mind is on the final level.

The earthly mind's reaction against the spiritual mind is also the reason the earthly mind consists of substances from the earthly world as well as substances from the spiritual world, as noted above. By their very nature, substances of the earthly world react against substances of the spiritual world, since substances of the earthly world are intrinsically dead and are activated from the outside by substances of the spiritual world. Anything that is dead and is activated from the outside resists by its very nature, and therefore reacts by its very nature.

We can tell from this that the earthly self reacts against the spiritual self, and that there is a conflict. It is all the same whether we refer to the earthly self and the spiritual self or to the earthly mind and the spiritual mind.

We can tell from this that if the spiritual mind is closed, the earthly mind is constantly resisting whatever comes from the spiritual mind, fearing that something from that source will flow in that will disturb its states. Everything that flows in through the spiritual mind is from heaven because the spiritual mind is a heaven in form; and everything that flows into the earthly mind is from the world because the earthly mind is a world in form. It follows, then, that when the spiritual mind is closed, the earthly mind resists everything that comes from heaven and will not let it in—except to the extent that it may serve as a means for gaining possession of worldly benefits. When heavenly things serve as means for the purposes of the earthly mind, then even though those means seem to be heavenly, they are still earthly. The purpose gives them their quality, and they actually become like items of information for the earthly self, items in which there is no trace of inner life.

However, since heavenly things cannot be united to earthly ones in this way so that they act as one, they distance themselves; and for people who are purely earthly, heavenly things come to rest outside, at the circumference, around the earthly things that are within. As a result, merely earthly people can discuss and preach heavenly things and can even act them out, even though they are thinking the opposite within. They behave one way when they are alone, and another way in public.

Because of an inborn reflex, the earthly mind or self resists what comes from the spiritual mind or self when that mind loves itself and the world above all else. Then it finds delight in all kinds of evil—in adultery, cheating, vindictiveness, blasphemy, and the like; and it also recognizes only nature as the creatress of the universe. It uses its rational ability to find proofs of all this, and once it has these proofs, it distorts or stifles or diverts whatever of the church and heaven is good and true. Eventually it either escapes such things, or rejects them, or hates them. It does this in spirit, and does it also physically whenever it dares to speak with others from its spirit without fear of losing reputation, for the sake of respectability and profit.

When people are like this, then their spiritual mind closes more and more tightly. It is primarily the justifications of evil by falsity that close it, which is why confirmed evil and falsity cannot be rooted out after death. They can be rooted out only in this world, by repentance.

When the spiritual mind is open, though, the state of the earthly mind is entirely different. Then the earthly mind is inclined to obey the spiritual mind and to be subservient. The spiritual mind acts on the earthly mind from above or from within; and it moves aside the things there that are reactive and adapts to its purposes the things that are cooperative. So it gradually eliminates any overpowering resistance.

We need to realize that action and reaction are involved in everything in the universe, no matter how large or small, whether alive or lifeless. This yields a balance throughout, which is canceled when action overcomes reaction or vice versa. It is the same for the earthly mind and the spiritual mind. When the earthly mind is acting on the basis of the delights it loves and the fascinations of its thinking (which are intrinsically evil and false), then the reaction of the earthly mind moves aside whatever comes from the spiritual mind and blocks the doors against its entry. As a result, any action is controlled by whatever agrees with the reaction. This is the nature of the action and reaction of the earthly mind, which is the opposite of the action and reaction of the spiritual mind; and this is what causes the closing of the spiritual mind or the reversing of the spiral.

However, if the spiritual mind is open, then the action and reaction of the earthly mind are reversed. The spiritual mind is acting from above or within, and as it does so it is working through whatever in the earthly mind is amenable, whether it comes from within or from the outside. Then it reverses the spiral characteristic of the action and reaction of the earthly mind. This mind has been in opposition to the purposes of the spiritual mind from birth, deriving this by heredity from our parents, as is well known.

This is the nature of that change of state called reformation and regeneration. The state of the earthly mind before its reformation might be compared to a spiral twisted or twisting downward, while after its reformation it might be compared to a spiral twisted or twisting upward. So before our reformation, we are looking down toward hell, while after our reformation we are looking up toward heaven.

 CREATION

The Word in the Old Testament contains secrets of heaven, and every single aspect of it has to do with the Lord, his heaven, the church, faith, and all the tenets of faith; but not a single person sees this in the letter. In the letter, or literal meaning, people see only that it deals for the most part with the external facts of the Jewish religion.

The truth is, however, that every part of the Old Testament holds an inner message. Except at a very few points, those inner depths never show on the surface. The exceptions are concepts that the Lord revealed and explained to the apostles, such as the fact that the sacrifices symbolize the Lord, and that the land of Canaan and Jerusalem symbolize heaven (which is why it is called the heavenly Canaan or Jerusalem [Galatians 4:26; Hebrews 11:16; 12:22; Revelation 21:2, 10]), as does paradise.

The Christian world, though, remains deeply ignorant of the fact that each and every detail down to the smallest—even down to the tiniest jot—enfolds and symbolizes spiritual and heavenly matters; and because it lacks such knowledge, it also lacks much interest in the Old Testament.

Still, Christians can come to a proper understanding if they reflect on a single notion: that since the Word is the Lord's and comes from him, it could not possibly exist unless it held within it the kinds of things that have to do with heaven, the church, and faith. Otherwise it could not be called the Lord's Word, nor could it be said to contain any life. Where, after all, does life come from if not from what is living? That is, if not from the fact that every single thing in the Word relates to the Lord, who is truly life itself? Whatever does not look to him at some deeper level, then, is without life; in fact, if a single expression in the Word does not embody or reflect him in its own way, it is not divine.

Without this interior life, the Word in its letter is dead. It resembles a human being, in that a human has an outward self and an inward one, as the Christian world knows. The outer being, separated from the inner, is just a body and so is dead, but the inward being is what lives and allows the outward being to live. The inner being is a person's soul.

In the same way, the letter of the Word by itself is a body without a soul.

The Word's literal meaning alone, when it monopolizes our thinking, can never provide a view of the inner contents. Take for example the first chapter of Genesis. The literal meaning by itself offers no clue that it is speaking of anything but the world's creation, the Garden of Eden (paradise), and Adam, the first human ever created. Who supposes anything else?

The wisdom hidden in these details (and never before revealed) will be clear enough from what follows. The inner sense of the first chapter of Genesis deals in general with the process that creates us anew—that is to say, with regeneration—and in particular with the very earliest church; and it does so in such a way that not even the smallest syllable fails to represent, symbolize, and incorporate this meaning.

But without the Lord's aid not a soul can possibly see that this is the case. As a result, it is proper to reveal in these pre-liminaries that the Lord in his divine mercy has granted me the opportunity for several years now, without break or interruption, to keep company with spirits and angels, to hear them talking, and to speak with them in turn. Consequently I have been able to see and hear the most amazing things in the other life, which have never before come into people's awareness or thought.

In that world I have been taught about the different kinds of spirits, the situation of souls after death, hell (or the regrettable state of the faithless), and heaven (or the blissful state of the faithful). In particular I have learned what is taught in the faith acknowledged by the whole of heaven. All of these topics will, with the Lord's divine mercy, be explored further in what follows. . . .

SUMMARY OF GENESIS 1

The six days or time periods [of Creation], meaning so many consecutive stages in a person's regeneration, are these, in outline:

The first stage is preliminary, extending from infancy to just before regeneration, and is called void, emptiness, and darkness. The first stirring, which is the Lord's mercy, is the Spirit of God in constant motion on the face of the water.

In the second stage, a distinction is drawn between the things that are the Lord's and those that are our own. The things that are the Lord's are called a "remnant" in the Word. In this instance the "remnant" refers principally to religious knowledge acquired from early childhood on. This remnant is stored away, not to reappear until we arrive at such a stage.

At present the second stage rarely comes into play without trouble, misfortune, and grief, which enable bodily and worldly concerns—things that are our own—to fade away and in effect die out. The things that belong to the outer self, then, are separated from those that belong to the inner self, the inner self containing the remnant that the Lord has put aside to await this time and this purpose.

The third stage is one of repentance. During this time, at the prompting of the inner self, we speak devoutly and reverently and yield a good harvest (acts of neighborly kindness, for instance). These effects are lifeless nonetheless, since we suppose that they come of our own doing. They are called the tender plant, then the seed-bearing plant, and lastly the fruit tree.

In the fourth stage, love stirs and faith enlightens us. Before this time we may have spoken devoutly and yielded a good harvest, but we did so in a state of trial and anguish, not at the call of faith and kindness. In consequence they are now kindled in our inner self and are called the two lights.

In the fifth stage, we *speak* with conviction and, in the process, strengthen ourselves in truth and goodness. The things we then produce have life in them and are called the fish of the sea and the birds in the heavens.

In the sixth stage, we *act* with conviction and therefore with love in speaking truth and doing good. What we then produce is called a living soul and a beast. Because we begin to act as much from love as from conviction, we become spiritual people, who are called [God's] image.

In regard to our *spiritual* lives, we now find pleasure and nourishment in religious knowledge and acts of kindness; and these are called our food. In regard to our *earthly* lives, we still find pleasure and sustenance in things relating to our body and our senses, which cause strife until love takes charge and we develop a heavenly character.

Not everyone who undergoes regeneration reaches this stage. Some (the great majority, these days) arrive only at the first stage, some only at the second, some at the third, fourth, or fifth, very few at the sixth, and almost no one at the seventh, [that of the heavenly person].

INNER MEANING

From this point on, the term *Lord* is used in only one way: to refer to the Savior of the world, Jesus Christ; and the name "Lord" is used without any additions.

He is acknowledged and revered as Lord throughout heaven because he possesses all power in heaven and on earth.

He also commanded this when he said, "You address me as 'Lord.' You speak correctly, because so I am" (John 13:13). And his disciples called him Lord after the resurrection.

In the whole of heaven no one knows of any other Father than the Lord, since the Father and the Lord are one. As he himself said:

> "I am the way and the truth and life." Philip says, "Show us the Father." Jesus says to him, "After all the time I've spent with you, don't you know me, Philip? Whoever has seen me has seen the Father. How then can you say, 'Show us the Father'? Don't you believe that I am in the Father and the Father is in me? Believe me, that I am in the Father and the Father is in me." (John 14:6, 8, 9, 10, 11)

Genesis 1:1. *In the beginning, God created heaven and earth.*

The word *beginning* is being used for the very earliest times. The prophets frequently call them "the days of old."

"The beginning" includes the first period of regeneration too, as that is when people are being born anew and receiving life. Because of this, regeneration itself is called our new creation [2 Corinthians 5:17; Galatians 6:15]. Almost everywhere in the prophetic books, the words *creating, forming,* and *making* stand for regenerating, though with differences. In Isaiah, for example:

> All have been called by my name, and I have created them for my glory; I have formed them; yes, I have made them. (Isaiah 43:7)

This is why the Lord is called Redeemer, One-Who-Forms-from-the-Womb, Maker, and Creator, as in the same prophet:

> I am Jehovah, your Holy One, the Creator of Israel, your Monarch. (Isaiah 43:15)

In David:

> The people created will praise Jah. (Psalms 102:18)

In the same author:

You send out your spirit—they will continue to be created—and you renew the face of the ground. (Psalms 104:30)

Heaven, or the sky, symbolizes the inner self, and the *earth,* before regeneration occurs, symbolizes the outer self, as may be seen below.

Genesis 1:2. *And the earth was void and emptiness, and there was darkness on the face of the abyss, and the Spirit of God was constantly moving on the face of the water.*

Before regeneration a person is called the *void, empty earth,* and also soil in which no seed of goodness or truth has been planted. *Void* refers to an absence of goodness and *empty* to an absence of truth. The result is *darkness,* in which a person is oblivious to or ignorant of anything having to do with faith in the Lord and consequently with a spiritual or heavenly life. The Lord portrays such a person this way in Jeremiah:

My people are dense; they do not know me. They are stupid children, without understanding. They are wise in doing evil but do not know how to do good. I looked at the *earth,* and there—void and emptiness; and to the *heavens,* and these had no light. (Jeremiah 4:22, 23, 25)

The *face of the abyss* means our cravings and the falsities these give rise to; we are wholly made up of cravings and falsities and wholly surrounded by them. Because no ray of light is in us, we are like an abyss, or something disorganized and dim.

Many passages in the Word also call such people abysses and sea depths, which are drained (that is, devastated) before a person is regenerated. In Isaiah, for instance:

Wake up, as in the days of old, the generations of eternity! Are you not draining the sea, the waters of the great abyss, and making the depths of the sea a path for the redeemed to cross? May those ransomed by Jehovah return! (Isaiah 51:9, 10, 11)

An individual of this type, observed from heaven, looks like a dark mass with no life at all to it.

The same words involve an individual's overall spiritual devastation—a preliminary step to regeneration. (The prophets have much more to say about it.) Before we can learn what is true and be affected by what is good, the things that stand in the way and resist have to be put aside. The old self must die before the new self can be conceived.

The *Spirit of God* stands for the Lord's mercy, which is portrayed as *moving constantly,* like a hen brooding over her eggs. What is being brooded over in this instance is what the Lord stores away in us, which throughout the Word is called "a remnant" [or "survivors"]. It is a knowledge of truth and goodness, which can never emerge into the light of day until our outer nature has been devastated. Such knowledge is here called the *face of the water.*

Genesis 1:3. *And God said, "Let there be light," and there was light.*

The first step is taken when we begin to realize that goodness and truth are something transcendent.

People who focus exclusively on externals do not even know what is good or what is true; everything connected with self-love and love of worldly advantages they consider good, and anything that promotes those two loves they consider true. They are unaware that such "goodness" is evil and such "truth" false.

When we are conceived anew, however, we first begin to be aware that our "good" is not good. And as we advance further into the light, it dawns on us that the Lord exists and that he is goodness and truth itself.

The Lord says in John that we need to know of his existence:

> Unless you believe that I am, you will die in your sins.
> (John 8:24)

We need to know too that the Lord is goodness itself, or life, and truth itself, or light, and consequently that nothing good or true exists that does not come from him. This is also found in John:

> In the beginning there was the Word, and the Word was present with God, and the Word was God. Everything was made by him, and nothing that was made was made without him. In him was life, and the life was the light of humankind; but the light appears in the darkness. He was the true light that shines on every person coming into the world. (John 1:1, 3, 4, [5,] 9)

Genesis 1:4, 5. *And God saw the light, that it was good, and God made a distinction between light and darkness. And God called the light day, and the darkness he called night.*

The *light* is said to be *good* because it is from the Lord, who is goodness itself.

The *darkness* is whatever looked like light to us before our new conception and birth, because we saw evil as good and falsity as truth; but it is actually darkness—our lingering sense of self-sufficiency.

Absolutely everything that is the Lord's is compared to the day, because it belongs to the light, and everything that is our own is compared to the night, because it belongs to the darkness. The Word draws this comparison in quite a few places.

Genesis 1:5. *And there was evening and there was morning, the first day.*

From this we now see what evening and morning mean. *Evening* is every preliminary stage, because such stages are marked by shadow, or by falsity and an absence of faith. *Morning* is all later stages, because these are marked by light, or by truth and religious knowledge.

Evening stands in general for everything that is our own, while morning stands for everything of the Lord's. As David says, for example:

> The Spirit of Jehovah has spoken in me and his words are on my tongue. The God of Israel has said, the rock of Israel has spoken to me. He is like the morning light when the sun rises, like a morning when there are no clouds, when because of the brightness, because of the rain, the tender grass springs from the earth. (2 Samuel 23:2, 3, 4)

Since evening is when there is no faith and morning is when there *is* faith, the Lord's coming into the world is called morning. The period in which he came, being a time of no faith, is called evening. In Daniel:

> The Holy One said to me, "Up till [the day's second] evening, when it becomes morning, two thousand and three hundred times." (Daniel 8:14, 26)

Morning in the Word is similarly taken to mean every coming of the Lord, so that it is a word for being created anew.

Nothing is more common in the Word than for a *day* to be understood as meaning the times, as in Isaiah:

> The day of Jehovah is near. Look—the day of Jehovah is coming! I will shake heaven, and the earth will tremble right out of its place, on the day when my anger blazes up. The time of his coming is near, and its days will not be postponed. (Isaiah 13:6, 9, 13, 22)

In the same prophet:

> In the days of old she was old. It will happen on that day that Tyre will be forgotten for seventy years, corresponding to the days of one king. (Isaiah 23:7, 15)

Because a day stands for a time period, it is also taken to mean the state we are in during that period, as in Jeremiah:

> Doom to us! For the day has faded, for the shadows of evening have lengthened. (Jeremiah 6:4)

In the same prophet:

> If you nullify my compact with the day and my compact with the night, so that there is no daytime or night at their times . . . (Jeremiah 33:20, 25)

And again:

> Renew our days as in ancient times. (Lamentations 5:21)

Genesis 1:6. *And God said, "Let there be an expanse in the middle of the waters, and let it exist to make a distinction among the waters, in the waters."*

The next step occurs after the Spirit of God—the Lord's mercy—brings out into daylight the knowledge of truth and goodness and provides the first glimmering that the Lord exists, that he is goodness and truth itself, and that nothing is good or true except what comes from him. The Spirit of God then *makes a distinction* between the inner and the outer being, and between the religious knowledge we possess in our inner selves and the secular knowledge belonging to our outer selves.

The inner self is called the *expanse,* the knowledge in the inner self is called the *waters over the expanse,* and the facts belonging to the outer self are called *the waters under the expanse.*

Before we are reborn, we do not know even that an inner being exists, let alone what it is, imagining there is no difference between the two selves. This is because we are absorbed by bodily and worldly interests and merge the concerns of the inner being with those interests. Out of distinct and separate planes we make one dim, confused whole.

Therefore this verse first says that there should be an expanse in the middle of the waters, then that it should exist to make a distinction "among the waters, in the waters," but not that it should make a distinction between one set of waters and another. The next verse says that.

Genesis 1:7, 8. *And God made the expanse, and he made a distinction between the waters that were under the expanse and the waters that were over the expanse, and so it was done; and God called the expanse heaven.*

The second thing we begin to notice while being reborn, then, is that the inner self exists. We become aware that the attributes of the inner self are good feelings and true ideas, which are the Lord's alone.

While we are being reborn, our outer self is such that it still believes we are acting on our own when we do what is good and speaking on our own when we speak what is true. The Lord uses those things—allowing them to seem like our own, since such is our mindset—to lead us to doing what is good and speaking what is true. Consequently we first learn to distinguish what is *under the expanse;* only then do we learn to distinguish what is *over the expanse.*

Another secret from heaven is that the Lord leads us by means of things that really are our own—both the illusions of our senses and our cravings—but diverts us toward things that are true and good. So every single moment of regeneration carries us forward from evening to morning, just as it takes us from the outer self to the inner, or from earth to heaven. This is why the expanse (the inner self) is now called *heaven.*

Spreading out the earth and stretching out the heavens is a customary formula used by the prophets when they speak of our regeneration. In Isaiah, for example:

This is what Jehovah has said, your Redeemer and the one who formed you from the womb: "I am Jehovah, making all things, stretching *the heavens* out on my own and spreading *the earth* out by myself." (Isaiah 44:24)

Again, where the Lord's Coming is spoken of openly:

> A crushed reed he does not break, and smoldering flax he does not quench; he propels judgment toward truth. [In other words, he does not break our illusions or extinguish our cravings but bends them toward truth and goodness. It continues:] God Jehovah creates *the heavens* and stretches them out. He spreads out *the earth* and the things it produces. He gives a soul to the people on it and spirit to everyone walking on it. (Isaiah 42:3, 4, 5)

Several other places could be cited as well.

Genesis 1:8. *And there was evening and there was morning, the second day.*

The meanings of *evening, morning,* and *day* are explained above at verse 5.

Genesis 1:9. *And God said, "Let the waters under heaven be gathered into one place, and let dry land appear"; and so it was done.*

When we learn that we have an inner self and an outer, and that truth and goodness come from the inner self—or rather from the Lord by way of the inner self into the outer, even though this is contrary to appearances—this information, this knowledge of truth and goodness, is stored away in our memory. The knowledge takes its place among the secular facts we have learned, because anything instilled in our outward memory, whether earthly, spiritual, or heavenly, lodges there as a fact, and from there the Lord draws on it.

This knowledge is the *waters gathered into one place* and named seas. The outer being itself, on the other hand, is called *dry land.* Immediately afterward it is called earth, as the next verse shows.

Genesis 1:10. *And God called the dry land earth, and the gathering of waters he called seas; and God saw that it was good.*

To find *waters* symbolizing religious and secular knowledge, and *seas* symbolizing a body of such knowledge, is quite common in the Word. In Isaiah:

The earth will be full with the awareness of Jehovah, like the waters covering the sea. (Isaiah 11:9)

In the same prophet, where both kinds of knowledge are portrayed as lacking:

The water will disappear from the sea, the river will drain away and dry up, and the streams will recede. (Isaiah 19:5, 6)

In Haggai, where a new church is the subject:

I am shaking *the heavens* and *the earth,* and the sea and the dry land; and I will shake all the nations, and those who are the desire of every nation will come, and I will fill this House with glory. (Haggai 2:6, 7)

And in Zechariah, on the regenerating individual:

That will be a single day; it is known to Jehovah; it is not *day* or night. And it will happen that at the time of *evening* there will be light. And it will happen on that day that living water will go out from Jerusalem, part of it to the eastern sea and part of it to the western sea. (Zechariah 14:7, 8)

In a passage in David depicting a devastated person who is being reborn and will come to revere the Lord:

Jehovah does not despise his prisoners; *the heavens* and *the earth,* the seas and every creeping thing in them will praise him. (Psalms 69:33, 34)

In the following passage in Zechariah, *the earth* symbolizes that which receives something put into it:

Jehovah is stretching out *the heavens* and founding *the earth* and forming the human spirit in the middle of it. (Zechariah 12:1)

Genesis 1:11, 12. And God said, "Let the earth cause the sprouting on the earth of the tender plant, of the plant bearing its seed, of the fruit tree making the fruit that holds its seed, each in the way of its kind"; and so it was done. And the earth produced the tender plant, the plant bearing its seed in the way of its kind, and the tree making the fruit that held its seed in the way of its kind. And God saw that it was good.

When the *earth* (a person) is so well prepared as to be able to accept heavenly seed from the Lord and to produce good and truth in some degree, that is the time when the Lord first *causes the sprouting* of something tender, called the *tender plant* or grass. Next he stimulates something more useful that reseeds itself—the *plant bearing its seed.* Finally he germinates something good, which reproduces fruitfully—the *tree making the fruit that holds its seed,* each of these *in the way of its kind.*

During regeneration we naturally suppose at first that the good we do and the truth we speak come from ourselves, when the reality is that all good and truth come from the Lord. If we imagine they come from ourselves, then, we are not yet in possession of the life force belonging to true faith (although we can receive it later). We cannot believe yet that they come from the Lord, because we are being prepared to receive the living power of faith. This stage is represented in the story by things that have no living soul; animate creatures represent the stage of living faith to come.

The Lord is the sower of seeds, the *seed* is his Word, and the *earth* is the human being, as he saw fit to say in Matthew 13:19–23, 37, 38, 39; Mark 4:14–20; and Luke 8:11–15. A similar description:

> So God's kingdom is like one who tosses seed into the earth and sleeps and rises night and day, and the seed sprouts and grows; how it happens, the person does not know. For the earth bears fruit readily—first a shoot, then an ear, then the full grain in the ear. (Mark 4:26, 27, 28)

"God's kingdom" in its broadest sense means the whole of heaven. Less broadly it means the Lord's true church. In its narrow sense it refers to everyone with true faith, which is to say, all who become reborn by living out their faith. Each of these people is also called a heaven (since they have heaven in them) and God's kingdom (since they have God's kingdom in them). The Lord himself teaches this in Luke:

> Jesus was asked by the Pharisees, "When is God's kingdom coming?" He answered them and said, "God's kingdom does not come in an observable way, nor will they say, 'Look here!' or 'Look there!' because—look!— God's kingdom is within you." (Luke 17:20, 21)

This is the third step in our regeneration and the stage at which we repent. The process continues to advance from shadow to light, from evening to morning, and so it says:

Genesis 1:13. *And there was evening and there was morning, the third day.*

Genesis 1:14, 15, 16, 17. *And God said, "Let there be lights in the expanse of the heavens to make a distinction between day and night; and they will act as signals and will be used for seasons for both the days and the years. And they will be lights in the expanse of the heavens, to shed light on the earth," and so it was done. And God made two great lights: the greater light to rule by day and the smaller light to rule by night; and the stars. And God placed them in the expanse of the heavens, to shed light on the earth.*

We cannot understand the identity of these great lights very well unless we first know what the essence of faith is and how it develops in those who are being created anew.

The actual essence and life of faith is the Lord alone. No one who lacks faith in the Lord can have life, as he himself said in John:

> Those who believe in the Son have eternal life, but those who do not believe in the Son will not see life; instead, God's anger will rest on them. (John 3:36)

The progress of faith in those who are being created anew is as follows. Initially such people are without any life, as no life exists in evil or falsity, only in goodness and truth. Afterward they receive life from the Lord through faith. The first form of faith to bring life is a memorized thing—a matter of fact. The next is faith that dwells in the understanding—faith truly understood. The last is faith in the heart, which is faith born of love, or saving faith.

In verses 3–13 the things that had no living soul represent factual faith and faith truly understood. Faith brought alive by love, however, is represented by the animate creatures in verses 20–25. Consequently this is the point at which love and the faith that rises out of it are first dealt with, and they are called *lights.* Love is the *greater light* that *rules by day;* faith springing from love is the *smaller light* that *rules by night.* And because they must unite as one, the verb used with "lights" is singular, "let it be" rather than "let them be."

Love and faith work the same way in our inner being as warmth and light work in our outer flesh and are therefore represented by warmth and light. This is why the lights are said to be *placed in the expanse of the heavens,* or our inner being, the greater light in our will and the smaller in our understanding. But they only seem to be present there, just as the light of the sun only appears to be in physical objects. It is the Lord's mercy alone that stirs our will with love and our understanding with truth or faith.

The fact that the *great lights* symbolize love and faith and that they are named sun, moon, and stars can be seen in many places in the prophets. In Ezekiel, for instance:

> When I blot you out I will cover *the heavens* and black out their stars; the sun I will cover with a cloud, and the moon will not make its light shine. All the lamps of light in the heavens I will black out above you, and I will bring shadow over your *land.* (Ezekiel 32:7, 8)

This passage is directed at Pharaoh and the Egyptians. In the Word, these people stand for sensory evidence and factual information, and the idea here is that they used both things to blot out love and faith. In Isaiah:

> The day of Jehovah [comes] to make *the earth* a desolation, since neither the stars of the heavens nor their Orions will shine their light. The sun has been shadowed over in its emergence, and the moon will not radiate its light. (Isaiah 13:9, 10)

In Joel:

> The day of Jehovah has come, a day of shadow and darkness. Before him the earth trembles, the heavens shake, the sun and moon turn black, and the stars hold back their rays. (Joel 2:1, 2, 10)

The following passage in Isaiah discusses the Lord's Coming and the light brought to the nations—in other words, a new church, and specifically the individuals who are in shadow but welcome the light and are being reborn.

Rise, shine, because your light has come! Look—shadows cover the earth, and darkness, the peoples. And Jehovah will dawn above you; and the nations will walk toward your light, and monarchs, toward the brightness of your rising. Jehovah will become an eternal light to you. No longer will your sun set, and your moon will not withdraw, because Jehovah will become an eternal light to you. (Isaiah 60:1, 2, 3, 19, 20)

In David:

Jehovah makes *the heavens* with understanding; he spreads *the earth* out on *the waters;* he makes the great lights—the sun to rule during the day and the moon and stars to rule during the night. (Psalms 136:5, 6, 7, 8, 9)

In the same author:

Give glory to Jehovah, sun and moon! Give glory to him, all you shining stars! Give glory to him, heavens of heavens and waters above the heavens! (Psalms 148:3, 4)

In all these places the sources of light symbolize love and faith.

Because lights represented and symbolized love for and faith in the Lord, the Jewish church was commanded to keep a light burning perpetually, from evening to morning, since every activity that was required of that church represented the Lord. The command for the perpetual light was as follows:

Command the children of Israel to take oil for the light, to make [the fire of] the lamp go up continually. In the meeting tent, outside the veil that is by [the ark of] the testimony, Aaron and his sons shall arrange it before Jehovah, from evening till morning. (Exodus 27:20, 21)

This symbolizes love and faith, which the Lord kindles and causes to shine in our inner self, and through our inner into our outer self.

Love and faith are first called the great lights; then love is called the *greater light* and faith the *smaller light*. It says that love will *rule during the day* and that faith will *rule during the night*. Because this information is unknown and less accessible than ever at this time—the end of an era—the Lord in his divine mercy has allowed me to lay open the true situation.

It is especially well hidden in these final days because the close of the age has arrived and almost no love exists, consequently almost no faith. The Lord himself predicted this event in words recorded in the Gospels:

> The sun will go dark, and the moon will not shed light, and the stars will fall down from the sky, and the powers of the heavens will be shaken. (Matthew 24:29)

The sun here means love, which has gone dark. The moon means faith, which is not shedding light. The stars mean religious concepts (the powers and forces of the heavens), which are falling down from heaven.

The earliest church acknowledged no faith besides love itself. Heavenly angels too have no idea what faith is if it is not a matter of love. The entirety of heaven gives itself over to love, because no other kind of life than that of love exists in the heavens. Love is the source of all their happiness, which is so immense that not a bit of it can be put into words or grasped in any way by the human mind.

People who dwell in love do love the Lord with all their heart, but they know, say, and perceive that all love comes from the Lord and from nowhere else, as does all life (which is the product of love alone) and so all happiness. Not the smallest measure of love, life, or happiness do they claim to possess on their own.

In the Lord's transfiguration, the great light—the sun—represented the fact that he is the source of all love, since

> His face shone like the sun, while his clothes became like the light. (Matthew 17:2)

The face symbolizes the deepest levels of being, while clothes symbolize the things that issue from those levels. So the sun (love) means the Lord's divinity, and light (the wisdom that rises out of love), his humanity.

Anyone can see perfectly well that no hint of life ever exists without some kind of love and that no trace of joy ever exists unless it results from love. The nature of the love determines the nature of the life and of the joy.

If you were to take the things you love—the things you long for (since longings are bound up with love)—and set them aside, your thought processes would come to an immediate halt and you would be like a corpse. I have learned this through experience.

Self-love and materialism produce an imitation of life and an imitation of joy, but since they are diametrically opposed to genuine love—that is, loving the Lord above all and loving our neighbor as ourselves—it stands to reason that they are not forms of love but of hatred. Notice that the more we love ourselves and worldly goods, the more we hate our neighbor and therefore the Lord.

Genuine love, then, is love for the Lord, and genuine life is a life of love received from him. True joy is the joy of that life.

Only one genuine love can exist, so only one genuine life can exist, and it gives rise to true joy and happiness, like that felt by angels in heaven.

Love and faith can never be separated, because they make a single unit. This is why the sources of light when first mentioned are treated as grammatically singular in the statement, "Let there be lights in the expanse of the heavens." Let me report some surprising facts in this connection.

Because the Lord gives heavenly angels this kind of love, love reveals all religious knowledge to them. Love also gives them such a living and shining intelligence that it can hardly be described.

For spirits who learn the doctrinal tenets of faith but lack love, on the other hand, life is so chill and the light so dim that they cannot even approach the near side of the threshold to heaven's entrance hall without fleeing in retreat.

Some say that they had believed in the Lord; but in actuality they had not lived as he taught. The Lord speaks of them this way in Matthew:

> Not everyone saying "Lord! Lord!" to me will enter the kingdom of the heavens, but the one doing my will. Many will say to me on that day, "Lord! Lord! Haven't we prophesied in your name?" (Matthew 7:21, 22)

See also what follows there, up to the end of Matthew 7.

All this makes it clear that people who have love also have faith and consequently heavenly life. The same cannot be said of those who claim to have faith but do not lead a loving life.

A life of faith without love is like sunlight without warmth— the type of light that occurs in winter, when nothing grows and everything droops and dies. Faith rising out of love, on the contrary, is like light from the sun in spring, when everything grows and flourishes. Warmth from the sun is the fertile agent. The same is true in spiritual and heavenly affairs, which are typically represented in the Word by objects found in nature and human culture.

Nonbelief and belief without love are in fact compared to winter by the Lord in Mark where he made predictions concerning the close of the age:

> Pray that your flight not occur in winter, as those will be days of distress. (Mark 13:18, 19)

The "flight" refers to the final days and to an individual's final days before death as well. "Winter" is a life devoid of love. The "days of distress" are the person's wretched condition in the other life.

Humans have two basic faculties: will and understanding. When the will regulates the understanding, the two together make one mind and as a result one life; under those circumstances, what we will and do is also what we think and intend. When the understanding is at odds with the will, though, as when we act in a way that contradicts what we claim to believe, our single mind is torn in two. One part wants to rise up to heaven while the other leans toward hell. And since the will drives everything, we would rush into hell heart and soul if the Lord did not take pity on us.

People who have separated faith from love do not even know what faith is. When they try to picture it, some see it merely as thought. Some view it only as thoughts about the Lord. A few equate it with the teachings of faith.

But faith is more than the knowledge and acknowledgment of all that is encompassed in the teachings of faith. First and foremost it is obedience to everything that faith teaches; and the primary thing faith teaches and requires our obedience to is love for the Lord and love for our neighbor. No one who lacks this possesses faith. The Lord teaches this so clearly in Mark that no one can doubt it.

> The first of all the commandments is "Listen, Israel: The Lord our God is one Lord. Therefore you shall love the Lord your God with all your heart and with all your soul and with all your mind and with all your powers." This is the first commandment. A second, similar one, of course, is this: "You shall love your neighbor as yourself." There is no other commandment greater than these. (Mark 12:28–34)

In Matthew he calls the former the first and great commandment and says that the Law and the Prophets depend on these commandments (Matthew 22:35–40). "The Law and the Prophets" are the teachings of faith, all-inclusively, and the whole Word.

The words *the lights will act as signals and will be used for seasons both for the days and for the years* contain more hidden information than can be spelled out in the present work, even though none of it appears in the literal meaning. The only thing to be said at this time is that spiritual and heavenly things—as a group and individually—go through cycles, for which the daily and yearly cycles are metaphors. The daily cycle begins in the morning, extends to midday, then to evening, and through night to morning. The corresponding annual cycle begins with spring, extends to summer, then to fall, and through winter to spring.

These changes create changes in temperature and light and in the earth's fertility, which are used as metaphors for changes in spiritual and heavenly conditions. Without change and variation, life would be monotonous and consequently lifeless. There would be no recognition or differentiation of goodness and truth, let alone any awareness of them.

The celestial cycles are called "statutes" in the prophets, as in Jeremiah:

> The word spoken by Jehovah, who gives the sun as light for the day, the statutes of moon and stars as light for the night: "These statutes will not depart from before me." (Jeremiah 31:35, 36)

And in the same prophet:

> This is what Jehovah has said: "If my compact with day and night should cease, if I should cease to set the statutes of heaven and earth . . ." (Jeremiah 33:25)

Genesis 1:18. . . . *and to rule during the day and during the night, and to make a distinction between light and darkness; and God saw that it was good.*

Day means goodness and *night* evil, so in common parlance the good things people do are associated with the day, while the bad things they do are called deeds of the night.

Light means truth and *darkness* falsity, as the Lord says:

People loved darkness more than light. One who does the truth comes to the light. (John 3:19–21)

Genesis 1:19. *And there was evening and there was morning, the fourth day.*

Genesis 1:20. *And God said, "Let the waters cause the creeping animal—a living soul—to creep out. And let the bird flit over the land, over the face of the expanse of the heavens."*

After the great lights are kindled and placed in the inner self, and the outer self is receiving light from them, the time arrives when we first start to live. Earlier, we can hardly be said to have been alive, thinking as we did that the good we perform and the truth we speak originate in ourselves. On our own we are dead and have nothing but evil and falsity inside, with the result that nothing we produce from ourselves has life. So true is this that by our own power we cannot do anything good—at least not anything inherently good.

From the doctrine taught by faith, anyone can see that we cannot so much as think a good thought or will a good result or consequently do a good deed except through the Lord's power. After all, in Matthew the Lord says:

The one who sows good seed is the Son of Humankind. (Matthew 13:37)

Good cannot come from anywhere but this same unique source, as he also says:

Nobody is good except the one God. (Luke 18:19)

Still, when the Lord brings us back to life, or regenerates us, he at first allows us to harbor these mistaken ideas. At that stage we cannot view the situation in any other way. Neither can we be led in any other way to believe and then perceive that everything good and true comes from the Lord alone.

As long as our thinking ran along these lines, the truth and goodness we possessed were equated with a tender plant or grass, next with a plant bearing seed, then with a fruit tree, none of which has a living soul. Now, when love and faith have brought us to life and we believe that the Lord brings about all the good we do and the truth we speak, we are compared initially to *creeping animals of the water* and *birds flitting over the land* and later to beasts. All these are animate and are called *living souls.*

The *creeping animals* that the *waters* breed symbolize facts that the outer self knows. *Birds* in general symbolize logical reasoning; they also symbolize matters that we truly understand, which belong to the inner self.

The following verses in Isaiah demonstrate the symbolism of the *creeping animals of the waters*—fish—as facts:

> I came and there was no man. In my censure I will dry
> up the sea; I will make the rivers a desert; their fish will
> stink from lack of water and die of thirst; I will dress
> the heavens in black. (Isaiah 50:2, 3)

Evidence still clearer appears in Ezekiel, where the Lord describes a new temple, the general meaning of which is a new church and an adherent of the church or person reborn (since everyone who is reborn is a temple to the Lord).

> The Lord Jehovah said to me, "That water, which will
> go out to the boundary toward the east and go toward
> the sea, will be channeled down into the sea, and the
> water [of the sea] will be cured. And it will come about
> that every living soul that creeps out in any place where
> the water of the rivers goes will survive; and the fish
> will be very numerous, because that water goes there
> and will be cured, and everything will live, wherever the
> river goes. And it will happen that the fishers will stand
> over it from En-gedi to En-eglaim; they will be there

spreading their nets. Their fish will be of all kinds, like the fish of the great sea, very numerous." (Ezekiel 47:8, 9, 10)

"Fishers from En-gedi to En-eglaim spreading their nets" symbolize people who are to teach the earthly plane of the human mind about the truths that make up faith.

Passages in the prophets establish the fact that birds symbolize logical reasoning and concepts truly understood. In Isaiah, for example:

> I am calling the winged creature from the sunrise, the man I planned on, from a faraway land. (Isaiah 46:11)

In Jeremiah:

> I looked and there, not a human! And every bird of the heavens had fled. (Jeremiah 4:25)

In Ezekiel:

> I will plant a cutting of the tall cedar, and it will lift its branch and make fruit and become a majestic cedar. And every bird of every wing will live under it; in the shade of its branches they will live. (Ezekiel 17:[22,] 23)

And in Hosea, where the subject is a new church, or the regenerate person:

> And I will strike a pact with them on that day—with the wild animal of the field, and with the bird in the heavens and the creature that moves on the ground. (Hosea 2:18)

The wild animal obviously does not mean a wild animal or the bird a bird, because the Lord is sealing a new pact with them.

Nothing that is a person's very own has any life in it. When presented to view, it looks hard as bone, and black. Everything that comes from the Lord, on the other hand, has life. It has a spiritual and heavenly quality and looks like something living and human.

Incredibly, perhaps (although it is absolutely true), each word, each mental image, and each scintilla of thought in an angelic spirit is alive. Passion received from the Lord, who is life itself, permeates every single thing about such a spirit.

Things that come from the Lord, then, contain life because they contain faith in him, and they are symbolized here by a *living soul*. Additionally, they have the equivalent of a physical body, symbolized by *that which moves* or *creeps*. This information remains obscure to the human mind, but since the verse talks about a living soul that moves, I need at least to mention it.

Genesis 1:21. *And God created the big sea creatures, and every living, creeping soul that the waters caused to creep out, in all their kinds, and every bird on the wing, of every kind; and God saw that it was good.*

Fish symbolize facts, as already stated. In this instance they symbolize facts animated by faith that is received from the Lord, which therefore possess vitality. *Big sea creatures* symbolize general categories of facts, from which come subcategories. (Not one thing exists anywhere in the world that does not belong to some general category. The category allows the particular item to come into being and continue in existence.)

The prophets mention sea monsters or whales a number of times, and when they do, these symbolize general categories of facts. Pharaoh, king of Egypt, representing human wisdom or understanding (that is, factual information in general), is called a large sea creature, as in Ezekiel:

> Here, now, I am against you, Pharaoh, king of Egypt, you great sea creature, lying in the middle of your rivers, who has said, "The river is mine, and I have made myself." (Ezekiel 29:3)

Another:

Raise a lamentation over Pharaoh, king of Egypt; and you are to tell him, "But you are like a monster in the seas; and you have emerged among your rivers and churned the waters with your feet." (Ezekiel 32:2)

This image symbolizes those who want to use facts (meaning they want to use their own powers) to initiate themselves into religious mysteries. In Isaiah:

On that day Jehovah, with his steely and great and mighty sword, will exact punishment on Leviathan the stretched-out serpent and on Leviathan the coiled serpent; and he will kill the monsters that are in the sea. (Isaiah 27:1)

Killing the monsters that are in the sea means leaving such people without awareness even of general facts. In Jeremiah:

Nebuchadnezzar, king of Babylon, has devoured me, has churned me up; he has rendered me an empty container, like a sea monster he has swallowed me down, filled his belly with the savors of me, hurled me out. (Jeremiah 51.34)

In other words, "Nebuchadnezzar" has swallowed up all religious knowledge (the "savors") as the sea monster did to Jonah. In Jonah's case the monster stood for people who possess the broad outlines of this knowledge in the form of facts and who wolf them down.

Genesis 1:22. *And God blessed them, saying, "Reproduce and multiply and fill the water in the seas, and the birds will multiply on the land."*
Everything with life from the Lord in it reproduces and multiplies beyond measure—not so much during our physical lives, but to an astounding degree in the next life.
In the Word, *reproducing* or being fruitful applies to the elements of love, and *multiplying*, to the elements of faith.

Fruit born of love holds the seed by which it multiplies so prolifically.

The Lord's *blessing* in the Word also symbolizes fruitfulness and multiplication, because these are its result.

Genesis 1:23. *And there was evening and there was morning, the fifth day.*

Genesis 1:24, 25. *And God said, "Let the earth produce each living soul according to its kind: the beast, and that which moves, and the wild animal of the earth, each according to its kind"; and so it was done. And God made each wild animal of the earth according to its kind, and each beast according to its kind, and every animal creeping on the ground according to its kind. And God saw that it was good.*

Like the earth, we are unable to produce any good unless we have first been sown with religious insights, which enable us to see what to believe and do.

The role of the understanding is to hear the Word, while the role of the will is to do it. To hear the Word and not act is to claim we believe it although we do not live by it. People who act like this separate the two and split their minds. The Lord says they are stupid:

> Everyone who hears my words and does them I compare to a prudent man who built his house on rock. But everyone who hears my words and does not do them I compare to a stupid man who built his house on sand. (Matthew 7:24, 26)

What the understanding grasps is symbolized, as shown, by creeping animals that the waters cause to creep out and birds flying over the land and over the face of the expanse. What the will is intent on is symbolized by the *living soul* that *the earth* is to *produce,* by the *beast* and *that which creeps,* and by the *wild animal of the earth.*

People who lived in the earliest times used the same kinds of symbols for the contents of the understanding and the will. In consequence, the different types of creature have a similar representation in the prophets and throughout the Old Testament Word.

Beasts are of two kinds: bad (because they are dangerous) and good (because they are tame). Bad animals—bears, wolves, and [feral] dogs, for instance—symbolize evil things in us. Good animals—young cattle, sheep, lambs—symbolize the good, gentle things in us. Because the present theme concerns people who are being reborn, the beasts in this verse are the good, tame ones, symbolizing feelings of affection.

The traits in us that belong to a lower order and rise more out of our body are called the wild animals of the earth; they are cravings and appetites.

Many examples from the Word can clarify the fact that *beasts* or animals symbolize the feelings we have—negative feelings if we are evil, positive feelings if we are good. Take these verses in Ezekiel:

> Here, now, I am yours, [mountains of Israel,] and I will turn to face you so that you may be tilled and sown; and I will multiply human and animal upon you, and they will multiply and reproduce; and I will cause you to live as in your ancient times. (Ezekiel 36:9, 10, 11)

This speaks of regeneration. In Joel:

> Do not be afraid, animals of my field; because the living-places of the desert have become grassy. (Joel 2:22)

In David:

> I was dull-witted; I was like the animals, in God's sight. (Psalms 73:22)

In Jeremiah:

Look! The days are coming when I will sow the house of Israel and the house of Judah with the seed of human and the seed of animal; and I will watch over them to build and to plant. (Jeremiah 31:27, 28)

This speaks of regeneration.

Wild animals have the same symbolism. In Hosea, for example:

I will strike a pact with them on that day—with the wild animal of the field, and with the bird in the heavens and the creeping animal of the earth. (Hosea 2:18)

In Job:

Of the wild animal of the earth you are not to be afraid, as you will have a compact with the stones of the field, and the wild animal of the field will be peaceful toward you. (Job 5:22, 23)

In Ezekiel:

I will strike a pact of peace with you and bring an end on the earth to the evil wild animal, so that people may live securely in the wilderness. (Ezekiel 34:25)

In Isaiah:

The wild animal of the field will honor me because I have put water in the desert. (Isaiah 43:20)

In Ezekiel:

In its branches nested every bird of the heavens, and under its branches bred every wild animal of the field, and in its shade lived all the great nations. (Ezekiel 31:6)

This describes Assyrians, who symbolize a person with a spiritual focus and who are being compared to the Garden of Eden. In David:

> Give glory to Jehovah, all you angels of his; give glory
> from the earth, you sea creatures, fruit tree, wild ani-
> mal, and every beast, creeping animal, and bird on the
> wing. (Psalms 148:2, 3, 4, 7, 9, 10)

This lists exactly the same things [as the present chapter]: sea creatures, fruit tree, wild animal, beast, creeping animal, and bird. Unless they symbolized living things in us, they could never be said to give glory to Jehovah.

The prophets draw a careful distinction between the animals *of the earth* and the animals of the field.

It is good things that have been called animals up to this point, just as the people closest to the Lord in heaven are termed living creatures both in Ezekiel [1; 10] and in John:

> All the angels stood around the throne and the elders
> and the four living creatures, and they fell down before
> the throne on their faces and worshiped the Lamb.
> (Revelation 7:11; 19:4)

People to whom the gospel is to be preached are also called created beings, since they are to be created anew:

> Go throughout the world and preach the gospel to
> every created being. (Mark 16:15)

More evidence that these words enfold the mysteries of regeneration can be seen in differences between the present verse and the last. The last says that the earth produced the living soul, the beast, and the wild animal of the earth. The present one employs a different order, saying that God made the wild animal of the earth and then the beast. At first we produce results as if on our own, as we do later, too, before developing a heavenly nature. Regeneration, then, starts with the outer self and moves to the inner, which is why a change in the order occurs, and outermost things come first.

All this verifies the premise: In the fifth stage we speak with conviction (an attribute of the understanding) and in the process strengthen ourselves in truth and goodness. The things we then produce have life in them and are called the fish of the sea and the birds in the heavens. And in the sixth stage we act with conviction (an attribute of the understanding) and therefore with love (an attribute of the will) in speaking truth and doing good. What we then produce is called a living soul, an animal. Because this is the point at which we begin to act as much with love as with conviction, we become spiritual people, who are called [God's] image—the very next subject.

Genesis 1:26. And God said, "Let us make a human in our image, after our likeness; and these will rule over the fish of the sea and over the bird in the heavens, and over the beast, and over all the earth, and over every creeping animal that creeps on the earth."

To members of the earliest church, whom the Lord addressed face to face, he appeared as a human being. (Many things could be told about these people, but this is not the right time.) As a consequence, they used the term *human* for none but him, or for his qualities. They did not even call themselves human, excepting whatever they could tell he gave them, such as all the good embraced by love and all the truth espoused by faith. These traits they described as human, because they were the Lord's.

As a consequence, the terms *human being* and *son of humankind* in the prophets have the Lord as their highest meaning. At a lower but still internal level, the meaning is wisdom and understanding and accordingly everyone who has been reborn. An example from Jeremiah:

> I looked at the earth, and there—void and emptiness; and to the heavens, and there—no light in them! I looked, and there—not a human! And all the birds of the heavens had fled. (Jeremiah 4:23, 25)

At the inner level, the following passage in Isaiah uses a human being to mean one reborn, and on the highest level the Lord himself, as an exemplar:

> This is what Jehovah, the Holy One of Israel and its fashioner, has said: "I made the earth, and the human being on it I created. My hands stretched out the heavens, and to their whole army I gave commands." (Isaiah 45:11, 12, 13)

For this reason, the prophets saw the Lord as a human being. Ezekiel was one who did:

> Above the expanse was a seeming appearance of sapphire stone, like a throne, and on the likeness of a throne was what looked like the appearance of a person on it, high above. (Ezekiel 1:26)

When Daniel saw the Lord, he called him "Son of Humankind," or human being, which is the same thing:

> I looked, and there! In the clouds of the sky, it was as if the Son of Humankind was coming, And he came to the Ancient One, and they brought him before [the Ancient One]. And he was given power to rule, and glory, and kingship; and all peoples, nations, and tongues will serve him. His ruling power is eternal, a power that will not pass away, and his kingship one that will not perish. (Daniel 7:13, 14)

In fact, the Lord often calls himself Son of Humankind, or human; echoing the prophecy in Daniel that he will come in glory, he says:

> They will see the Son of Humankind coming in the clouds of the sky with strength and glory. (Matthew 24:27, 30)

"The clouds of the heavens" (or sky) is what the literal meaning of the Word is called. "Strength and glory" are terms for the Word's inner meaning, which at each and every point focuses exclusively on the Lord and his kingdom. This focus is what gives the inner meaning strength and glory.

What the people of the earliest church meant when they spoke of the Lord's *image* involves more than can be put into words.

People have no idea whatever that the Lord governs them through angels and spirits, or that at least two spirits and two angels accompany each of them. The spirits create a link with the world of spirits, and the angels create one with heaven. We cannot possibly live without a channel of communication open to the world of spirits through spirits and to heaven through angels (and in this way to the Lord through heaven). Our life depends totally on such a connection. If the spirits and angels withdrew from us, we would be destroyed in a second.

As long as we are unregenerate, we are governed in a completely different way than the regenerate. Before regeneration we have with us evil spirits whose grip on us is so strong that the angels, though present, can achieve hardly any results. All they can do is head us off from rushing into the worst kind of evil and divert us toward some form of good. They even use our own appetites to lead us toward good, and the illusions of our senses to lead us toward truth. Under these circumstances we communicate with the world of spirits by means of the spirits around us but not so much with heaven, since the evil spirits are in charge and the angels only deflect their influence.

When we are regenerate, on the other hand, the angels are in charge, inspiring us with all kinds of goodness and truth and instilling a horror and fear of evil and falsity.

Angels do give us guidance, but they are mere helpers; the Lord alone governs us, *through* angels and spirits. Since angels have their assisting role, the words of this verse appear in the plural—"Let us make a human in our image." But since only the Lord rules and manages us, the next verse uses the singular—"God created the human in his image." The Lord states his role clearly in Isaiah:

> This is what Jehovah has said, your Redeemer and the one who formed you from the womb: "I, Jehovah, make all things, stretching *the heavens* out on my own, spreading *the earth* out by myself." (Isaiah 44:24)

The angels themselves confess that they have no power but act only at the Lord's behest.

As far as an *image* is concerned, it is not the likeness of another thing but is *after a likeness* of it, which explains the wording "Let us make a human in our image, after our likeness." A person with a spiritual character is an image, but a person with a heavenly character is a likeness or exact copy. Genesis 1 deals with the spiritual person, Genesis 2 with the heavenly person.

The Lord calls the person of spiritual character (or an "image") a child of light, as he does in John:

> Those who walk in the dark do not know where they are heading. As long as you have the light, believe in the light, in order to be children of light. (John 12:35, 36)

He also calls such a person a friend:

> You are my friends if you do whatever I command you. (John 15:14, 15)

But the person of heavenly character (or a "likeness") he calls God's child in John:

> As many as did accept him, to them he gave the power to be God's children, to those believing in his name, who had their birth not from blood or from the flesh's will or from a man's will but from God. (John 1:12, 13)

As long as we are spiritual, we rule the outer self first and from this the inner, as illustrated here in Genesis 1:26: *and they will rule over the fish of the sea and over the bird in the heavens, and over the beast, and over all the earth, and over every creeping animal that creeps on the earth.* When we become heavenly, though, and do good because we love to, we rule the inner self first and from it the outer. The Lord describes this as being true of himself; and as it is true of him, it is also true of the heavenly type of person, who is a likeness of him. The words appear in David:

> You have made him rule over the works of your hands;
> all things you have put under his feet: the flock and all
> the herds, and also the animals of the fields, the bird
> in the heavens, and the fish of the sea—that which
> travels the paths of the seas. (Psalms 8:6–8)

In this passage, animals receive the first mention, next the bird, then the fish of the sea, because the heavenly person proceeds from love, which belongs to the will. Things are different with the spiritual person, for whom the fish and birds come first and the animals follow; fish and birds are associated with the understanding, which concerns itself with faith.

Genesis 1:27. *And God created the human in his image; in God's image he created them.*

Image comes up twice in this verse because faith, which belongs to the understanding, is called *his* image, but love, which belongs to the will, is called *God's* image. Love comes second in the spiritual person but first in the heavenly person.

Male and female he created them.

The inner meaning of male and female was very familiar to the earliest church, although their successors lost touch with this secret when they lost sight of any deeper import to the Word.

These earliest people found their greatest happiness and pleasure in marriage. Whenever they could possibly draw a comparison between something else and marriage, they did so, in order to perceive the happiness of marriage in that other entity. Being people of depth, they enjoyed only the deeper aspects of things. External objects were just for looking at; their thoughts were occupied instead with the things those objects represented. External objects, then, were nothing to them, serving only as a springboard for reflection on inner realities, and these for contemplation of heavenly realities and so of the Lord, who was everything to them. The same process caused them to reflect on the heavenly marriage, which they could tell was the source of the happiness in their own marriages.

As a result, they called the understanding in the spiritual being *male* and the will there *female;* and when the two worked together, they called it a marriage.

That religion initiated the practice, which became quite common, of calling the church Daughter or Virgin (as in "the Virgin Zion," "the Virgin Jerusalem") and also Wife, on account of its desire for good.

Genesis 1:28. *And God blessed them, and God said to them, "Reproduce and multiply, and fill the earth and harness it, and rule over the fish of the sea and over the bird in the heavens and over every living animal creeping on the earth."*

The earliest people called the interconnection of understanding and will or of faith and love a marriage, so the generation of any good from that marriage they termed *reproduction,* and the generation of any truth they termed *multiplication.* Because they did so, the prophets did so too; in Ezekiel, for instance:

> I will multiply human and animal upon you, [mountains of Israel,] and they will multiply and reproduce; and I will cause you to live as in your ancient times. And I will do good to you beyond that at your beginnings, and you will know that I am Jehovah. And I will

cause *humankind*—my people Israel—to walk upon you. (Ezekiel 36:8, 9, 10, 11, 12)

Humankind here means the spiritual being, which is also called Israel; the ancient times mean the very earliest church; and the beginnings mean the ancient church, which followed the Flood. The multiplying (of truth) comes before the reproducing (of good) because these verses describe the person who is being reborn, not the one who has been reborn already.

When the understanding couples with the will in us, or faith with love, the Lord through Isaiah calls us a married land:

No longer will your land be named Devastated; but you will be called I Am Well Pleased with Her, and your land, Married, since Jehovah will take pleasure in you. And your land will be married. (Isaiah 62:4)

The fruits of truth produced by this marriage are called sons, while the fruits of goodness are called daughters, as occurs quite often in the Word.

The *earth is filled* when truth and goodness proliferate, because when the Lord *blesses* and *says things* (that is, operates), goodness and truth grow beyond measure. As he states:

The kingdom of the heavens is like a mustard seed that you have taken and sown in your field, which to be sure is the smallest of all the seeds; but when it has grown, it is bigger than all the plants and becomes a tree, so that the birds of the sky come and nest in its branches. (Matthew 13:31, 32)

The mustard seed is the good we have before developing a spiritual orientation; it is the smallest of all the seeds, because we suppose that we do good on our own. Anything we do on our own is evil through and through, but since we are engaged in the process of being reborn, we have a trace—the smallest possible trace—of goodness. Later, as faith becomes more closely connected with love, it grows larger—a plant. When the connection is completed, it turns into a tree, and then the birds of the heavens (which here as before are true ideas, or the contents of the understanding) nest in its branches (the facts we know).

When we are spiritual people or are becoming spiritual, we are subject to conflict; and this is why it says *harness the earth, and rule.*

Genesis 1:29. *And God said, "Here, now, I am giving you every seed-bearing plant on the face of all the earth and every tree that has fruit; the tree that produces seed will serve you for food."*

A person whose nature is heavenly enjoys only heavenly things, which are called heavenly food because they harmonize with the life such a person lives. A person whose nature is spiritual enjoys spiritual things, which are called spiritual food because they harmonize with the life this person lives. A person focused on the physical world similarly enjoys earthly things, which are called food because they are vital to such a person; these are mainly facts.

As spiritual people are the subject at present, their spiritual food is depicted by the representative items here. *The seed-bearing plant* represents a spiritual type of this food, as does *the tree that has fruit;* the more general term for both is *the tree that produces seed.* These people's earthly food is described in the next verse.

The seed-bearing plant is every true idea that looks toward a useful goal. *The tree that has fruit* is religious good; the fruit is what the Lord gives the heavenly person, but the seed leading to new fruit is what he gives the spiritual person, which is why it says *the tree that produces seed will serve you for food.*

The next chapter, [*Secrets of Heaven* §§66-136], treating of the heavenly type of person, will demonstrate that heavenly food is called the fruit from a tree. Here the Lord's words through Ezekiel will suffice:

Beside the river, on its bank, on this side and that, grows every food tree. Its leaf will not fall, and its fruit will not be used up. Month by month it is reborn, because its waters are going out from the sanctuary. And its fruit will serve as food, and its leaf, as medicine. (Ezekiel 47:12)

"Water from the sanctuary" symbolizes the living energy and mercy of the Lord, who is the "sanctuary." The fruit symbolizes wisdom, which is food to people of heavenly character. The leaf is intelligence, which is given to them for a purpose referred to as "medicine."

The idea that spiritual food is called a plant (or grass), though, is expressed in David:

My shepherd, I will lack nothing. In grassy pastures you make me lie down. (Psalms 23:1, 2)

Genesis 1:30. *"And every wild animal of the earth and every bird in the heavens and every animal creeping on the earth, in which there is a living soul—every green plant will serve them for nourishment"; and so it was done.*

This verse depicts the spiritual person's earthly food. The *wild animal of the earth* symbolizes such a person's earthly plane of existence, as does the *bird in the heavens,* both of which received *for nourishment* the *green plant* or grass. Concerning this person's two kinds of food—both earthly and spiritual—David has the following to say:

Jehovah causes grain to sprout for the beast and plants for the service of humankind, to bring bread from the earth. (Psalms 104:14)

"The beast" stands for the wild animal of the earth and at the same time for the bird in the heavens, both of which David mentions in verses 11 and 12 of the same Psalm.

In this verse the nourishment of the earthly self is restricted to *green plants* for the following reason.

While we are being reborn and learning to concern ourselves with the spirit, we are in constant battle (which is why the Lord's church is described as militant). Up to this point our cravings have controlled us, because our whole being is cobbled together out of nothing but those cravings and the distorted ideas they spawn. We cannot rid ourselves of those longings and distortions instantaneously during regeneration; to do so would destroy us completely, since we have not yet acquired another way of life. Consequently, evil spirits are left with us for a long time to trigger our appetites, which then break down in countless different ways, and break down so thoroughly that the Lord can turn them into something good. This is the way we reform.

In the time of battle, evil spirits leave us no other nourishment than the equivalent of green plants. (Those spirits hold an absolute hatred for everything good and true—for anything having to do with love for the Lord and faith in him, these being the only good and true things that exist—because such things hold eternal life within them.) But from time to time the Lord gives us additional food that can be compared to seed-bearing plants and fruit trees: calm and peace, with their accompanying joy and happiness.

If the Lord were not protecting us every moment, every split second, we would be wiped out instantly. Hatred against any aspect of love for the Lord or faith in him dominates the world of spirits, and the hatred is so deadly that it defies description.

I can testify to the truth of this absolutely. For several years now I have visited the next world and the spirits there, though remaining in my body, and the evil ones (the worst, in fact) have crowded around me, sometimes numbering in the thousands. They have been allowed to spew out their venom and harass me in every possible way, but still they were unable to hurt a single hair on my head, so closely did the Lord guard me.

All these years of experience have taught me a great deal about the nature of the world of spirits and about the conflict that those who are being reborn inevitably suffer if they are to win the happiness of eternal life.

No one, however, can learn enough from a general description to develop an unshakable belief in this information, so the details, with the Lord's divine mercy, must come [in the parts of *Secrets of Heaven* that follow].

Genesis 1:31. *And God saw all that he had done and, yes, it was very good. And there was evening and there was morning, the sixth day.*

This time it says *very good* but previously it said simply *good*, because now the components of faith combine with those of love to make one entity. A marriage between spiritual and heavenly things has taken place.

"Spiritual" is the adjective for anything having to do with religious knowledge. "Heavenly" applies to everything having to do with love for the Lord and for our neighbor. Spiritual things fall in the province of our understanding; heavenly things, in that of our will.

The periods and stages of our regeneration—both the whole process and individual cycles within it—divide into *six,* and these six are called our days of creation. Step by step we advance from being nonhuman to being somewhat human, though only a little, then more and more so up to the sixth day, when we become [God's] image.

All the while the Lord is constantly fighting on our behalf against evil and falsity and through these battles strengthens us in truth and goodness. The time of conflict is when the Lord is at work (for which reason the prophets call a regenerate person the work of God's fingers [Psalms 8:3, 6; Isaiah 19:25; 29:23;

45:11; 60:21; 64:8; Lamentations 4:2]), and he does not rest until love takes the lead. Then the conflict ends.

When the work progresses so far that faith is united with love, it is called *very good,* since the Lord now makes us likenesses of himself.

At the end of the sixth day, evil spirits retreat and good ones take their place. We are led into heaven, or the paradise of heaven.

ABOUT EMANUEL SWEDENBORG

Emanuel Swedenborg (1688–1772) was born Emanuel Swedberg (or Svedberg) in Stockholm, Sweden, on January 29, 1688 (Julian calendar). He was the third of the nine children of Jesper Swedberg (1653–1735) and Sara Behm (1666–1696). At the age of eight he lost his mother. After the death of his only older brother ten days later, he became the oldest living son. In 1697 his father married Sara Bergia (1666–1720), who developed great affection for Emanuel and left him a significant inheritance. His father, a Lutheran clergyman, later became a celebrated and controversial bishop, whose diocese included the Swedish churches in Pennsylvania and in London, England.

After studying at the University of Uppsala (1699–1709), Emanuel journeyed to England, Holland, France, and Germany (1710–1715) to study and work with leading scientists in western Europe. Upon his return he apprenticed as an engineer under the brilliant Swedish inventor Christopher Polhem (1661–1751). He gained favor with Sweden's King Charles XII (1682–1718), who gave him a salaried position as an overseer of Sweden's mining industry (1716–1747). Although he was engaged, he never married.

After the death of Charles XII, Emanuel was ennobled by Queen Ulrika Eleonora (1688–1741), and his last name was changed to Swedenborg (or Svedenborg). This change in status gave him a seat in the Swedish House of Nobles, where he remained an active participant in the Swedish government throughout his life.

A member of the Royal Swedish Academy of Sciences, he devoted himself to scientific studies and philosophical reflections that culminated in a number of publications, most notably a comprehensive three-volume work on mineralogy (1734) that brought him recognition across Europe as a scientist and philosopher. After 1734 he redirected his research and publishing to a study of anatomy in search of the interface between the soul and body, making several significant discoveries in physiology.

From 1743 to 1745 he entered a transitional phase that resulted in a shift of his main focus from science and philosophy to theology. Throughout the rest of his life he maintained that this shift was brought about by Jesus Christ, who appeared to him, called him to a new mission, and opened his perception to a permanent dual consciousness of this life and the life after death.

He devoted the last decades of his life to studying Scripture and publishing eighteen theological titles that draw on the Bible, reasoning, and his own spiritual experiences. These works present a Christian theology with unique perspectives on the nature of God, the spiritual world, the Bible, the human mind, and the path to salvation.

Swedenborg died in London on March 29, 1772, at the age of eighty-four.